Say It Right in THAI

Easily Pronounced Language Systems

Clyde Peters

New York Chicago San Francisco Lisbon London Madrid Mexico City
Milan New Delhi San Juan Seoul Singapore Sydney Toronto

The *McGraw·Hill* Companies

1 2 3 4 5 6 7 8 9 10 11 12 13 14 15   WFR/WFR   1 9 8 7 6 5 4 3 2 1 0

ISBN 978-0-07-166434-9
MHID   0-07-166434-3

Library of Congress Cataloging-in-Publication Data

Peters, Clyde.
        Say it right in Thai / Clyde Peters, Author.
                p.   cm. (Say it right)
        Includes index.
        ISBN 0-07-166434-3 (alk. paper)
        1. Thai language—Textbooks for foreign speakers—English.   2. Thai language—
Conversation and phrase books—English.   3. Thai language—Spoken Thai.
I. Easily pronounced language systems.   II. Series.

PL4163 .P48   2010
495.9'183421—dc22

                                                                            2010016512

Also available: *Say It Right in Arabic* • *Say It Right in Brazilian Portuguese* • *Say It Right in Chinese* • *Say It Right in Chinese, Audio Edition* • *Say It Right in Dutch* • *Say It Right in French* • *Say It Right in French, Audio Edition* • *Say It Right in German* • *Say It Right in Greek* • *Say It Right in Italian* • *Say It Right in Italian, Audio Edition* • *Say It Right in Japanese* • *Say It Right in Korean* • *Say It Right in Russian* • *Say It Right in Spanish* • *Say It Right in Spanish, Audio Edition* • *Dígalo correctamente en inglés [Say It Right in English]*

Author: Clyde Peters
Illustrations: Luc Nisset
President, EPLS: Betty Chapman, www.isayitright.com
Senior Series Editor: Priscilla Leal Bailey
Thai Language Consultant: Suwsa Suwanlamai

McGraw-Hill books are available at special quantity discounts to use as premiums and sales promotions or for use in corporate training programs. To contact a representative, please e-mail us at bulksales@mcgraw-hill.com.

This book is printed on acid-free paper.

CONTENTS

INTRODUCTION

The SAY IT RIGHT FOREIGN LANGUAGE PHRASE BOOK SERIES has been developed with the conviction that learning to speak a foreign language should be fun and easy!

All SAY IT RIGHT phrase books feature the EPLS Vowel Symbol System, a revolutionary phonetic system that stresses consistency, clarity, and above all, simplicity!

Since this unique phonetic system is used in all SAY IT RIGHT phrase books, you only have to learn the VOWEL SYMBOL SYSTEM ONCE!

The SAY IT RIGHT series uses the easiest phrases possible for English speakers to pronounce and is designed to reflect how foreign languages are used by native speakers.

You will be amazed at how confidence in your pronunciation leads to an eagerness to talk to other people in their own language.

Whether you want to learn a new language for travel, education, business, study, or personal enrichment, SAY IT RIGHT phrase books offer a simple and effective method of pronunciation and communication.

PRONUNCIATION GUIDE

Most English speakers are familiar with the Thai word **Thai.** This is how the correct pronunciation is represented in the EPLS Vowel Symbol System.

All Thai vowel sounds are assigned a specific non-changing symbol. When these symbols are used in conjunction with consonants and read normally, pronunciation of even the most difficult foreign word becomes incredibly EASY!

On the following page are all the EPLS vowel Symbols used in this book. They are EASY to LEARN since their sounds are familiar. Beneath each symbol are three English words which contain the sound of the symbol.

Practice pronouncing the words under each symbol until you mentally associate the correct vowel sound with the correct symbol. Most symbols are pronounced the way they look!

THE SAME BASIC SYMBOLS ARE USED IN ALL SAY IT RIGHT PHRASE BOOKS!

EPLS VOWEL SYMBOL SYSTEM

(A)
Ace
Bake
Safe

(EE)
See
Feet
Meet

(I)
Ice
Kite
Pie

(O)
Oak
Cold
Sold

(oo)
Cool
Pool
Too

(ĕ)
Men
Red
Bed

(ă)
Cat
Sad
Hat

(ah)
Calm
Saw
Law

(i)
Win
Give
Lift

(uh)
Sun
Fun
Run

(Ur)
Hurt
Turn
Burn

(ou)
Would
Could
Cook

(oy)
Toy
Joy
Boy

(ow)
Cow
Now
How

(ew)
Few
New
Dew

(A) *
Clay
Stay
Way

*Elongated Symbols: Many of the symbols on this page will appear in oval form. This is a simple way to remind you to stretch this sound slightly.

EPLS VOWEL SYMBOL ENHANCEMENT

We begin with the EPLS Vowel Symbols, then EPLS enhances those symbols to visually demonstrate the sound e.g., regular, elongated, and tones (shown below). This visual EPLS enhancement makes it easy for you to perfect your Thai accent and enjoy the variety of sounds that make up the beautiful sing-song language of Thailand.

Literal translation in Thai is very different from the actual English phrases in this book. The reason is because Thai language uses the least number of words to convey or express a thought.

In Thai each word has built-in tones. (See page x for more detail.) You must practice these tones in order to be understood. They can not be dismissed as each tone is integrated in the meaning of the word.

Below is a small graph that visually demonstrates each tone. Move your hand like a music conductor and follow across the line pronouncing the letter A. Start with your normal voice called the "mid" tone and follow the key chart.

Mid	High	Low	Rising	Falling	Stretch
Ⓐ	Ⓐ	Ⓐ	Ⓐ	Ⓐ	Ⓐ

(Notice that the high and low symbols sit slightly above and below the lines respectively.)

EPLS CONSONANTS

The following pronunciation guide letters represent unique Thai consonant sounds.

K̞   Pronounce this **EPLS** letter very lightly like the **ch** in the Scottish word lo**ch**.

R̞   Pronounce like the rolled Spanish **r**.

H̋   Pronounce this **EPLS** letter like the **h** in "**ha**" preceded by a puff of air making an aspirated **H** sound.

CH Pronounced like the **ch** in the word **ch**air.

NY There is no sound in English that represents the Thai letters "**ng**" when used in the initial position in Thai. EPLS uses **NY** to represent the sound made by the "**ni**" voiced in the word Virgi**ni**a and o**ni**on. Note: The letters **NG** are pronounced normally like the **ng** in the word si**ng**.

P̲   This **EPLS** letter represents two Thai letters "**bp**" which sound is not found in the English language. It is somewhere between the **p** in **p**eas and **b** in **b**eef in English. Say the word **b**louse and notice how the lips purse and there is no air. Now purse your lips and say **p** in the same way with no air and you will have an idea how to pronounce the **bp** sound.

T̲   This letter is pronounced somewhere between the hard **t** in the **t**ime and the hard **d** in **d**ime and represents the letters "**dt**" in Thai.

TONES

Thai is a syllabic language and tones are inherently built in and determine the meaning of words. This is well demonstrated on page 22 "Useful Opposites," pronunciation for the words "**near**" and "**far**." You will see how the EPLS Vowel Symbol System makes tones easy by providing a visual enhancement for high, low, rising, falling and mid tones. (See page viii.)

Mid tone is spoken at an ordinary pitch without inflection and is represented by basic vowel symbols.

Come

Maa

M(ah)

High tone reflects a high pitch. The EPLS symbol sits above the syllable to visually illustrate this.

Small

Lek

L(ĕ)K

Low tone is spoken at a lower pitch than **mid** tone. The EPLS symbol sits lower than the regular letters in the syllable.

To keep

Gep

G(ĕ)P

The **rising** tone is accomplished by a rising inflection similar to asking a question in English. The EPLS symbol tilts upward to visually illustrate this.

Three

Saam

S(ah)M

The **falling** tone is similar to a glottal stop! This symbol simply tilts downward.

Rice

Kao

K(ow)

PRONUNCIATION TIPS

- Each pronunciation guide word is broken into syllables. Read each word slowly, one syllable at a time, increasing speed as you become more familiar with the system.

- Absolute Rule: In Thai it is important to make a conscious effort to add Khrap/Kha after a phrase. Khrap is always spoken by a male and Kha is spoken by female. This makes the sentence or phrase less abrupt and is very important to the language without question.

- In Thai the tone is built into the word and is integral to the meaning.

- To perfect your Thai accent and tones, you must listen closely to Thai speakers and adjust your speech accordingly. In the beginning you should try to exaggerate the tonal sound.

- It should be said here that although Thai is a tonal language, as are Chinese and Vietnamese, there is no connection between these languages.

- Additionally, some Thai words are spelled and pronounced exactly the same and the meaning is dictated by the context. An example of this is on page 22 "Useful Opposites."

- The pronunciation choices in this book were chosen for their simplicity and effectiveness.

ICONS USED IN THIS BOOK

KEY WORDS

You will find this icon at the beginning of chapters indicating key words relating to chapter content. These are important words to become familiar with.

PHRASEMAKER

The Phrasemaker icon provides the traveler with a choice of phrases that allows the user to make his or her own sentences.

Say It Right in
THAI

ESSENTIAL WORDS AND PHRASES

Here are some basic words and phrases that will help you express your needs and feelings in **Thai**.

Hello
สวัสดี

S@h-W@hD-D@   (♂ KR@P   ♀ K@h)

How are you?
สบายดีไหม?

S@h-B@ D@ M@   (♂ KR@P   ♀ K@h)

Very good, thanks.
สบายดีมาก ขอบคุณ

S@h-B@ D@-M@K K@P KH@N
                    (♂ KR@P   ♀ K@h)

---

*A Brief Note on Polite Particles (Absolute Rule)

Most Thai phrases should be made more polite by adding a particle to the end. Male speakers should add (khrap) while female speakers should add (kha). You will see the symbols below throughout the book to remind you of the correct way to end your phrase. The male and female symbols shown here are placed by each phrase on pages 2 and 3 to demonstrate and remind you to use them consistently.

(m) Masculine: (♂) KR@P
(f) Feminine: (♀) K@h

Good morning

สวัสดี

S⒜-W⒜D-D㏄   (♂ KR⒜P   ♀ K⒜)

Good afternoon

สวัสดี

S⒜-W⒜D-D㏄   (♂ KR⒜P   ♀ K⒜)

Good evening

สวัสดี

S⒜-W⒜D-D㏄   (♂ KR⒜P   ♀ K⒜)

Good night

ราตรีสวัสดิ์

R⒜-DTR㏄ S⒜-W⒜D   (♂ KR⒜P   ♀ K⒜)

See you later

แล้วพบกันใหม่

L⒜O P○P G⒜N M①   (♂ KR⒜P   ♀ K⒜)

Good-bye (polite)

ลาก่อน

L⒜-G○N   (♂ KR⒜P   ♀ K⒜)

Good-bye (informal)

ไปก่อนนะ

P①-G○N-N⒜   (♂ KR⒜P   ♀ K⒜)

Yes

ใช่

CHØ

No

ไม่

MØ

OK

โอเค

Ⓞ-KⒶ

Please

ช่วย

CHⓄⓄⒾ

Thank you

ขอบคุณ

KⓐP KᴴⓄⓄN

I'm sorry. / Excuse me.

ฉันขอโทษ

CHⓐN KⓄ-TⓄT   (♦) KBⓐP (♦) Kⓐh

I don't understand.

ฉันไม่เข้าใจ

Man speaking: (POM) MO KOW JO

Woman speaking: (DI-CHAN) MO KOW JO

Do you understand?

คุณเข้าใจไหม?

KHOON KOW JO MO

I'm a tourist.

ฉันเป็นนักท่องเที่ยว

CHAN PEN NAK TONG TEEOW

I can't speak Thai.

ฉันพูดภาษาไทยไม่ได้

CHAN POT Pah-SAH
TO MO DO

Do you speak English?

คุณพูดภาษาอังกฤษได้ไหม?

KHOON POT Pah-SAH
AhNG-GROT DO MO

Please repeat.

พูดอีกที

POT EEK TEE

FEELINGS

In Thai **I** or **me** can be pronounced three
different ways depending on whether you
are male or female. A man speaking would say P⊙M,
a woman speaking would say D㊉-CH⊛N and both can
use CH⊛N. All three uses are shown below. On the next
page phrases are shown using the neutral CH⊛N.

I would like...   CH⊛N Y⊛K J⊛...
ฉันอยากจะ...

Man speaking: (P⊙M) Y⊛K J⊛...KR⊛P

Woman speaking: (D㊉-CH⊛N) Y⊛K J⊛...K⊛

I want / need... CH⊛N T⊘NG G⊛N...
ฉันต้องการ...

Man speaking: (P⊙M) T⊘NG G⊛N...KR⊛P

Woman speaking: (D㊉-CH⊛N) T⊘NG G⊛N...K⊛

I have...   CH⊛N M㊉...
ฉันมี...

Man speaking: (P⊙M) M㊉...KR⊛P

Woman speaking: (D㊉-CH⊛N) M㊉...K⊛

I don't have... CH⊛N M⊘ M㊉...
ฉันไม่มี...

Man speaking: (P⊙M) M⊘ M㊉...KR⊛P

Woman speaking: (D㊉-CH⊛N) M⊘ M㊉...K⊛

I'm lost.

ฉันหลงทาง

CHⒶN LⓄNG-TⒶNG

We are lost.

เราหลงทาง

RⓄW LⓄNG-TⒶNG

I'm tired.

ฉันเหนื่อย

CHⒶN NⓄⒶ

I'm ill.

ฉันไม่สบาย

CHⒶN MⓄ-SⒶ-BⒾ

I'm hungry.

ฉันหิว

CHⒶN HⓄW

I'm thirsty.

ฉันหิวน้ำ

CHⒶN HⓄW-NⒶM

I'm happy.

ฉันมีความสุข

CHⒶN MEE-KWⒶM-SⓄK

CHⒶN is both neutral and informal for I or me.

INTRODUCTIONS

Use the following phrases when meeting someone for the first time, both privately and in business.

Man speaking

Hello

สวัสดีครับ

S(ah)-W(ah)D-D(EE)-KR(ah)P

My name is...

ผมชื่อ...ครับ

P(O)M CH(oo) (your name here) KR(ah)P

Very nice to meet you.

ยินดีที่พบคุณครับ

Y(i)N D(EE) T(EE)

P(O)P KH(oo)N KR(ah)P

ABSOLUTE RULE: In Thai it is important to make a conscious effort to add ครับ KR(ah)P / คะ K(ah) after a phrase. Khrap is always spoken by a male and Kha is spoken. by female. This makes the sentence or phrase less abrupt and is very important to the language without question.

(m) Masculine: (🚹) KR(ah)P
(f) Feminine: (🚺) K(ah)

Woman speaking

Hello

สวัสดีค่ะ

S⒜-W⒜D-D㋍-K⒜

My name is…

ดิฉันชื่อ… ค่ะ

D⒤-CH⒜N CH㋐ (your name here) K⒜

Very nice to meet you.

ยินดีที่พบคุณค่ะ

Y⒤N D㋍ T㋍
P⓪P KH㋐N-K⒜

Thailand is known as "The Land of Smiles" as well as a country that places great importance on respect. This is demonstrated every day in the way people talk to one another. As a traveler you will not be expected to know and use every nuance of the language, but your attempts to speak Thai will be greatly appreciated.

The WAI greeting is the standard greeting in Thailand. It is accomplished by putting hands together, bringing them up to the chest while slightly bowing, and just touching the nose with your closed palms. It is a sign of respect shown to those who are older or of higher social status.

THE BIG QUESTIONS

Who?

ใคร?

KRI

Who is it?

ใคร?

KRI

What?

อะไร?

ah-RI

What is this?

นี่คืออะไร?

NEE   Koo   ah-RI

When?

เมื่อไหร่?

Moo-ah-RI

Where?

ที่ไหน?

TEE-NI

Where is…?

…อยู่ที่ไหน?

…Y⓪ Tⓔⓔ N①

Which?

อันไหน?

ⓐⓗN-N①

Why?

ทำไม?

TⓐⓗM-M①

How?

อย่างไร?

YⓐⓗNG-ℝ①

How long?

นานเท่าไร?

NⓐⓗN-Tⓞⓦ-ℝ①

How much? (money)

เท่าไร?

Tⓞⓦ-ℝ①

ASKING FOR THINGS

The following phrases are valuable for directions, food, help, etc.

I would like…

ฉันอยากจะ...

CH@N Y@K J@h...

I need…

ฉันต้องการ...

CH@N T@NG G@N...

KOR is the Thai equivalent of the polite way of saying "Please give me" or "May I ask."

May I ask?
ฉันขอถามได้ไหม?

CH@N KO T@M DO MO

Thank you.
ขอบคุณ

K@P KH@N

PHRASEMAKER

Combine **"I would like"** with
the following phrases **beneath**
it and you will have a good idea
how to **ask** for things.

I would like…
ฉันอยากจะ…

CH@N Y@K J@…

▸ **coffee**

กาแฟ

G@-F@

▸ **some water**

น้ำ

N@M

▸ **ice water**

น้ำเย็น

N@M Y@N

▸ **the menu**

รายการอาหาร

R@-G@N-@-H@N

PHRASEMAKER

Here are a few sentences
you can use when you feel the
urge to say **I need**... or **can you**...?

I need...

ฉันต้องการ...

CH@N T@NG G@hN... (♦) KR@P (♦) K@h

▶ **your help**

ความช่วยเหลือของคุณ

KW@M CH@I L@-L@h K@NG KH@N

▶ **directions**

ทิศทาง

T@T T@hNG

▶ **change** (money)

แลกเงิน

L@K NY@N

▶ **a doctor**

หมอ

M@

▶ **a lawyer**

ทนายความ

T@h-N@ KW@M

PHRASEMAKER

Can you...

คุณช่วย...

KʰOON CHOOI... (♦) KR@P (♦) K@h

▸ **help me?**

ฉันได้ไหม?

CH@N DO MO

▸ **give me?**

...ให้ฉันได้ไหม?

...HO CH@N DO MO

▸ **tell me...?**

บอกฉันได้ไหมว่า...?

BOK CH@N DO MO W@...

▸ **take me to...?**

พาฉันไป (...) ได้ไหม?

P@h CH@N PO (place)

DO MO

ASKING THE WAY

No matter how independent you are, sooner or later you'll probably have to ask for directions.

Where is…?

…อยู่ที่ไหน?

…Y⓪⓪ T⓺⓺ N①

Name what you are looking for first.

I'm looking for…

ฉันกำลังมองหา…

CHⓐN GⓐM-LⓐNG MⓐNG Hⓐ…

Which way?

ทางไหน?

TⓐNG N①

I need directions.

ฉันต้องการรู้ทางไป

CHⓐN TⓐNG GⓐN R⓪⓪ TⓐNG B①

I'm lost!

ฉันหลงทาง!

CHⓐN L①NG TⓐNG

PHRASEMAKER

To say **Where is...?**, name what
you are looking for then go to the
bottom of the page and say...Y⓪ T☺ N①

▸ **Restroom...**
ห้องน้ำ...

H⓪NG-NⓐⓗM...

▸ **Telephone...**
โทรศัพท์...

TO-Ŗⓐⓗ-SⓐⓗP...

▸ **Beach...**
ชายหาด...

CH①-HⓐⓗT...

▸ **Hotel...**
โรงแรม...

ŖONG-Ŗⓐⓜ...

▸ **The train for...**
รถไฟที่ไป...

ŖⓄT F① T☺ P① (name where) ...

...where is it?
...อยู่ที่ไหน?

...Y⓪ T☺ N①

TIME

What time is it?

เวลาเท่าไหร่แล้ว?

WA Lah TOW RI Lāew

Morning

ตอนเช้า

TahN-CHOW

Noon

เที่ยงวัน

TEEahNG-WahN

Today

วันนี้

WahN-NEE

Tomorrow

พรุ่งนี้

PROONG-NEE

This week
อาทิตย์นี้

ah-TⓘT-NⒺⒺ

This month
เดือนนี้

DⓄⓊⓐⓗN-NⒺⒺ

This year
ปีนี้

PⒺⒺ-NⒺⒺ

Now
เดี๋ยวนี้

DⒺⒺⓄⓌ-NⒺⒺ

Soon
เร็วเร็วนี้

RⒺⓄ-RⒺⓄ-NⒺⒺ

Later
ทีหลัง

TⒺⒺ-LⓐNG

Never
ไม่เคย

MⓄ-KⓄⓊⒺⒺ

WHO IS IT?

I / me (man speaking)

ผม

P**O**M

I / me (woman speaking)

ดิฉัน

D**i**-CH**an**N

I / me (man or woman speaking)

ฉัน

CH**an**N

You (plural)

พวกคุณ

P**oo**ahK-K**h**oo**N

He / she

เขา

K**ow**

We

เรา

R**ow**

They

พวกเขา

P**oo**ahK-K**ow**

THIS AND THAT

The equivalents of **this, that,** and **these** are as follows:

This
นี่

N

This is mine.
นี่ของฉัน

N KONG CHON

That
นั่น

NON

That is mine.
นั่นของฉัน

NON KONG CHON

These
เหล่านี้

Low-N

These are mine.
เหล่านี้เป็นของฉัน

Low-N PEN KONG CHON

USEFUL OPPOSITES

Hot	**Cold**
ร้อน	หนาว
R@hN	N@w
Here	**There**
ที่นี่	ที่นั่น
T@@-N@@	T@@-N@@N
Near	**Far**
ไกล้	ใกล
GL@	GL@
Left	**Right**
ซ้าย	ขวา
S@	KW@
A little	**A lot**
นิดหน่อย	มาก
N@T-N@y	M@K
More	**Less**
มากขึ้น	น้อยลง
M@K-K@N	N@y-L@NG

Big	**Small**
ใหญ่	เล็ก
Y⓵	LⓔK
Open	**Closed**
เปิด	ปิด
ⓊⓇD	P⓵T
Cheap	**Expensive**
ถูก	แพง
T⓪⓪K	PⓐNG
Clean	**Dirty**
สะอาด	สกปรก
S⓪-⓪D	S⓪-G⓪-PR⓪K
Good	**Bad**
ดี	เลว
DⒺⒺ	Lⓐ⓪
Right (correct)	**Wrong**
ถูก	ผิด
T⓪⓪K	P⓵T

A word can be pronounced the same but the meaning changes in the context of the sentence where it is used. For example look at the pronunciation for the words "**cheap**" and "**right**."

WORDS OF ENDEARMENT

I like you.

ฉันชอบคุณ

CH**an** CH**ah**B K**h**OON

I love you.

ผมรักคุณครับ / ดิฉันรักคุณค่ะ

P**O**M R**ah**K K**h**OON KR**ah**P (man to woman)

D**i**-CH**an** R**ah**K K**h**OON K**ah** (woman to man)

I miss you.

ผมคิดถึงคุณครับ / ดิฉันคิดถึงคุณค่ะ

(man to woman)

P**O**M K**i**T T**oo**NG K**h**OON KR**ah**P

(woman to man)

D**i**-CH**an** K**i**T T**oo**NG K**h**OON K**ah**

I love Bangkok.

ฉันรักกรุงเทพฯ

CH**an** R**ah**K GR**oo**NG-T**o**P

I love Thailand.

ฉันรักประเทศไทย

CH**an** R**ah**K PR**ah** T**o**T T**i**

WORDS OF ANGER

Go away!

ไป!

PI

Stop bothering me!

หยุด!

Y00T R0B G@N CH@N

What do you want?

คุณต้องการอะไร?

KʰOON T@NG G@N @h-RI

Be quiet!

กรุณาเงียบ!

G@h-R00-N@h N@@P

Leave me alone!

อย่ามายุ่งกับฉัน!

Y@h M@h Y00NG
G@P CH@N

COMMON EXPRESSIONS

When you are at a loss for words but have the feeling you should say something, try one of these!

No problem.
ไม่มีปัญหา

MO-MEE-PahN-Hah

Congratulations!
ยินดีด้วย!

YiN-DEE-DOOI

Good luck!
โชคดี!

CHOK-DEE

Welcome!
ยินดีต้อนรับ!

YiN-DEE-TahN-Rahp

Cheers! (Past tense: action has occurred)
ไชโย!

CHI-YO

Great!

เยี่ยม!

Y@@@M

What a shame! / That's too bad.

แย่จัง

Y@ J@NG

Wonderful!

เลิศ!

L@T

Fantastic!

วิเศษ!

W①-S@T

USEFUL COMMANDS

Stop!

หยุด!

Y(oo)T

Go!

ไป!

P(I)

Wait!

รอ!

R(O)

Hurry!

รีบ รีบ!

R(ee)P-R(ee)P

Slow down!

ช้าลง!

CH(ah)-L(O)NG

Come here!

มาที่นี่!

M(ah)-T(ee)-N(ee)

EMERGENCIES

Fire!

ไฟไหม้!

F①-M⓪

Help!

ช่วยด้วย!

CH⓪①-D⓪①

Emergency!

เหตุฉุกเฉิน!

HⓔT-CH⓪K-CH⓪N

Call the police!

ตามตำรวจ!

TⓐM TⓐM-R⓪ⓐT

Call a doctor!

ตามหมอหน่อย!

TⓐM-M⓪-N⓪y

Call an ambulance!

ตามรถพยาบาล!

TⓐM R⓪T Pⓐh-Yⓐh-BⓐN

ARRIVAL

Passing through customs should be easy since there are usually agents available who speak English. You may be asked how long you intend to stay and if you have anything to declare.

- Have your passport ready.

- Be sure all documents are up to date.

- Time in Thiland is broken down into four segments of time in a 24 hour clock. This is confusing to travelers and it is best to just use the 24-hour clock that you are used to.

- While in a foreign country, it is wise to keep receipts for everything you buy.

- Be aware that many countries will charge a departure tax when you leave. Your travel agent should be able to find out if this affects you.

- If you have connecting flights, be sure to reconfirm them in advance.

- Make sure your luggage is clearly marked inside and out and always keep an eye on it when in public places.

- Take valuables and medicines in carry-on bags.

KEY WORDS

Baggage

กระเป๋าเดินทาง

GRah-Pow-DUN-Tahng

Customs

ศุลกากร

Soo-Lah-Gah-GON

Documents

เอกสาร

eK-Gah-Sahn

Passport

หนังสือเดินทาง

Nahng-Soo-DUN-Tahng

Security

ยาม

Yahm

Tax

ภาษี

Pah-See

USEFUL PHRASES

Here is my passport.

นี่คือหนังสือเดินทางของฉัน

NEE KOO NANG-SOU DUN
TANG KONG CHON

I have nothing to declare.

ไม่มีอะไรที่จะสำแดง

MO MEE ah-RI TEE Jah
SOM DANG

I'm here on business.

ฉันมาธุระ

CHON Mah TOO-Rah

I'm on vacation.

ฉันมาพักผ่อน

CHON Mah POK PON

Is there a problem?

มีปัญหาไหม?

MEE PON Hah MO

PHRASEMAKER

I'll be staying…

ฉันจะพัก…

CH**ah**N J**ah** P**ah**… (👤) KR**ah**P (👤) K**ah**

▸ **one night**
หนึ่งคืน

N**oo**NG-K**oo**N

▸ **two nights**
สองคืน

S**O**NG-K**oo**N

▸ **one week**
หนึ่งอาทิตย์

N**oo**NG-**ah**-T**i**T

▸ **two weeks**
สองอาทิตย์

S**O**NG-**ah**-T**i**T

USEFUL PHRASES

I need a porter.

ขอคนยกกระเป๋า

KŌ KŌN YŌK
GRah-POW

These are my bags.

เหล่านี้คือกระเป๋าของฉัน

Low NEE Kou GRah-POW
KŌNG CHĀN

I'm missing a bag.

กระเป๋าของฉันหา

GRah-POW KŌNG
CHĀN HŌ

Thank you. This is for you.

ขอบคุณ นี่สำหรับคุณ

KahP KHOON
NEE SĀM BahP KHOON

PHRASEMAKER

To say **Where is...?**, name
what you are looking for then go to
the bottom of the page and say...Y㋐ T㋔ N①

▶ **Customs...**

ศุลกากร...

S㋐-L㋐-G㋐-G①N...

▶ **Baggage claim...**

ที่รับกระเป๋า...

T㋔ R㋐P GR㋐-P㋜...

▶ **The money exchange...**

แลกเปลี่ยนเงิน...

T㋔ L㋐K PL㋓㋐N NY㋜N...

▶ **The taxi stand...**

ที่จอดรถแท็กซี่...

T㋔ JOT R①T T㋐K-S㋔...

▶ **The bus stop...**

ป้ายรถเมย์...

P② R①T M㋐...

...where is?

...อยู่ที่ไหน?

...Y㋐ T㋔ N①

HOTEL SURVIVAL

A wide selection of accommodations is available in Bangkok. You can find good values overall from guest bed reservations right up to the Oriental Hotel.

- Make reservations well in advance and and get written confirmation of your reservation before you leave home.

- Do not leave valuables or cash in your room when you are not there!

- Electrical items like blow-dryers may be provided by your hotel, however, you may want to purchase small electrical appliances there.

- It is a good idea to make sure you give your room number to persons you expect to call you. This can avoid confusion with Western names.

KEY WORDS

Hotel

โรงแรม

RONG-RAM

Bellman

พนักงานเปิดประตู

Pah-NahK-NYahN-PooD-PRah-Too

Maid

พนักงานทำความสะอาด

Pah-NahK-NYahN-TahM
KWahM-Sah-ahT

Message

ข้อความ

KO-KWahM

Reservation

การจอง

GahN-JONG

Room service

แผนกบริการ

Pah-NehK BO-REE-GahN

CHECKING IN

My name is…

ฉันชื่อ…

CH⟨a⟩N CH⟨oo⟩… (♦) KR⟨a⟩P (♦) K⟨a⟩h

I have a reservation.

ฉันจองมาแล้ว

CH⟨a⟩N J⟨O⟩NG
M⟨a⟩h L⟨a⟩⟨ow⟩

Have you any vacancies?

มีห้องว่างไหม?

M⟨EE⟩ H⟨O⟩NG W⟨a⟩NG M⟨I⟩

What is the charge per night?

ค่าห้องราคาคืนละเท่าไหร่?

K⟨a⟩ H⟨O⟩NG B⟨a⟩h-K⟨a⟩h
K⟨OO⟩N L⟨a⟩h T⟨ow⟩-R⟨I⟩

Is there room service?

ที่นั่นมีแผนกบริการไหม?

T⟨EE⟩ N⟨a⟩N M⟨EE⟩ P⟨a⟩h-N⟨e⟩K
B⟨O⟩-R⟨EE⟩-G⟨a⟩N M⟨I⟩

PHRASEMAKER

I would like a room with…
ฉันอยากจะได้ห้องที่มี…

CH@N Y@K J@ D@
H@NG T@ M@... (♦) KR@P (♦) K@

▶ **a bath**
อ่างอาบน้ำ

@NG-@P-N@M

▶ **one bed**
เตียงเดี่ยว

T_EE@NG D@@W

▶ **two beds**
เตียงคู่

T_EE@NG K@

▶ **a shower**
ฝักบัว

F@K B@@

USEFUL PHRASES

My room key, please.

ขอกุญแจห้อง

KO KʰOON-Jâ HÓNG

Are there any messages for me?

มีข้อความถึงฉันไหม?

MEE KO-KWâM TŎNG
CHâN MI

Where is the dining room?

ห้องทานอาหารเย็นอยู่ที่ไหน?

HÓNG TâN âh-HŎN
YÊN YOO TEE NI

Are meals included?

รวมอาหารเช้าไหม?

ROOâM âh-HŎN CHOW MÓ

What time is breakfast?

อาหารเช้าจัดกี่โมง?

âh-HŎN CHOW JâT
GEE MONG

PHRASEMAKER
(WAKE UP CALL)

Please wake me at…

กรุณาปลุกฉันเวลา...

G@h-R@@-N@h PL@@K CH@N W@ L@h...

▶ **6:00 AM**

หกโมงเช้า

H@K M@NG CH@

▶ **6:30 AM**

หกโมงครึ่งตอนเช้า

H@K M@NG KR@NG T@N CH@

▶ **7:00 AM**

เจ็ดโมงเช้า

J@T M@NG CH@

▶ **7:30 AM**

เจ็ดโมงครึ่งตอนเช้า

J@T M@NG KR@NG T@N CH@

▶ **8:00 AM**

แปดโมงเช้า

P@T M@NG CH@

(♂) KR@P   (♀) K@h

PHRASEMAKER

I need…

ฉันต้องการ ...

CH@N T@NG G@N... (♦) KR@P (♦) K@

▸ **a babysitter**

พี่เลี้ยงเด็ก

P@-L@@@NG-D@K

▸ **a bellman**

พนักงานเปิดประตู

P@-N@K-NY@N-P@D-PR@-T@@

▸ **a hotel safe**

ตู้เซฟ

T@@ S@F

▸ **a maid**

พนักงานทำความสะอาด

P@-N@K-NY@N-T@M

KW@M-S@-@T

▸ **the manager**

ผู้จัดการ

P@@-J@T-G@N

▶ **an extra key**

กุญแจเสริม

GOON-JǍ-SOOM

▶ **clean sheets**

ผ้าปูที่นอน

P̲ah̲-P̲oo-TEE-NON

▶ **ice cubes**

น้ำแข็ง

Nah̲M-KǍNG

▶ **more blankets**

ผ้าห่มอีก

P̲ah̲-HoM EEK

▶ **more towels**

ผ้าเช็ดตัวอีก

P̲ah̲-CHĔT-Tooah̲ EEK

▶ **soap**

สบู่

Sah̲-Boo

▶ **toilet paper**

กระดาษชำระ

GRah̲-Dah̲T CHah̲M Rah̲

(♂) KRah̲P (♀) Kah̲

PHRASEMAKER

(PROBLEMS)

There is no…
ไม่มี…

M⃝ MEE… (♦) KB⍺P (♦) K⍺

▶ **electricity**
ไฟฟ้า

F⃝-F⍺

▶ **hot water**
น้ำร้อน

N⍺M B⃝N

▶ **light**
ไฟ

F⃝

▶ **toilet paper**
กระดาษชำระ

GB⍺-D⍺T CH⍺M-B⍺

PHRASEMAKER

(SPECIAL NEEDS)

Do you have…

คุณมี…

KHⓄN MⒺⒺ… (♦) KRⓐP (♦) Kⓐh

▸ **an elevator?**

มีลิฟท์ไหม?

MⒺⒺ-LⓘP-MⓄ

▸ **a ramp?**

ทางลาด?

TⓐNG-LⓐⓉ

▸ **a wheel chair?**

รถเข็น?

RⓄT-KⒺN

▸ **facilities for the disabled?**

สิ่งอำนวยความสะดวกสำหรับคนพิการ?

SⓘNG ⓐM-NⓄⓄⒶ KWⓐM ⓘ

Sⓐh-DⓄⓄⓐK SⓐM RⓐP KⓄN

Pⓘ-GⓐN

CHECKING OUT

The bill, please.

เช็คบิล

CH̄ĒK B̄IN

Is this bill correct?

บิลนี้ถูกหรือเปล่า?

B̄IN N̄EE T̄OOK R̄OU PL̄OW

Do you accept credit cards?

รับบัตรเครดิตไหม?

R̄AP B̄AHT KR̄E-D̄IT M̄I

Could you have my luggage brought down?

คุณช่วยขนกระเป๋าของฉันได้ไหม?

KH̄OON CH̄OOI K̄ON
KR̄AH-P̄OW K̄ONG
CH̄AN D̄O M̄I

Please call a taxi.

กรุณาเรียกแท็กซี่

Kah-Roo-Nah Reeak
Tak-See

I had a very good time!

ฉันมีช่วงเวลาที่ดีมาก มาก!

Chan Mee Chooang
Wa-Lah Tee Dee
Mahk-Mahk

Thanks for everything.

ขอบคุณสำหรับทุกอย่าง

Kop Khoon Sahm-Rap
Took-Yang

We'll see you next time.

แล้วพบกันใหม่

Laow Pop Gahn Mi

Good-bye. (informal)

ลาก่อน

Lah-Gon

RESTAURANT SURVIVAL

Thai cuisine is a wonderful combination of Eastern and Western influences combined into uniquely Thai dishes. Thai food is very popular worldwide.

- There are many options for great eating from a variety of upscale restaurants including a fusion of Thai and Western cuisine. There are also the usual brand name fast food restaurants as well.

- Tap water is not suitable for drinking.

- Khao San Road is a great place to dip into Thai culture, culinary delights, and nightlife as well as the limitless shopping that Thailand has to offer.

KEY WORDS

Breakfast

อาหารเช้า

@-H@N-CH@

Lunch

อาหารกลางวัน

@-H@N-GL@NG-W@N

Dinner

อาหารเย็น

@-H@N-Y@N

Waiter

น้อง

N@NG   (♦) KB@P (♦) K@

Waitress

น้อง

N@NG   (♦) KB@P (♦) K@

Restaurant

ร้านอาหาร

B@N-@-H@N

USEFUL PHRASES

The menu, please.

ขอรายการอาหาร

KO RI GahN
ah-HaN

Separate checks, please.

แยกบิล

YaK BON

We are in a hurry.

เรากำลังรีบ

Row GahM LahNG Rep

What do you recommend?

คุณมีอะไรแนะนำบ้าง?

KHooN-MEE ah-RI
Na-NahM BoNG

Please bring me / us…

ขอ...หน่อย

KO...Noy (♂) KRap (♀) Kah

I'm hungry.

ฉันหิว

CHaN Hew

I'm thirsty.

ฉันหิวน้ำ

CHaN Hew NahM

Is service included?

รวมค่าบริการหรือยัง?

ROOaM Kah BO-REE-KahN ROO YahNG

The bill, please.

เช็คบิล

CHeK BiN

THAI CUISINES AND STYLES

Thai food is known for its balance of five fundamental flavors in each dish or the overall meal: hot (spicy), sour, sweet, salty, and (optional) bitter.

Meals consist of several dishes surrounding a main dish of rice (khao) sitting in the center of the Thai table. Normally there are more side dishes served than there are guests at the table.

Knives are not used at traditional Thai tables. Food is eaten using forks and spoons, using the fork to get the food on the spoon which is held by the right hand.

K©R is the Thai equivalent of the polite way of saying "Please bring me" or "May I ask." N⊚y is also added for politeness and means Lit: (little).

Please bring me...

ขอ...หน่อย

K©...N⊚y

Some Famous Thai Dishes:

Khao pat (KOW-PahT)
You will find this dish everywhere as it is most common in Thailand. Thai fried rice usually contains one or more but not limited to, ingredients of chicken, beef, shrimp, or pork.

Khanom jeen namya (Kah-NOM-JEEN NahM-Yah)
These rice noodles are round and are prepared by boiling. They are served with a fish-based sauce.

Khao khluk kapi (KOW-KLOOK-Gah-PEE)
This dish consists of rice stir-fried in a shrimp paste with pork and vegetables.

Khao man kai (KOW-MahN-GI)
Rice steamed with garlic with boiled chicken, chicken stock, and a dipping sauce.

Khao pat kai (KOW-PahT GI)
Fried rice with chicken.

Tom ka kai (TOM Kah GI)
Popular chicken and mushroom soup.

BEVERAGE LIST

Coffee

กาแฟ

G**ah**-F**ě**

Decaffeinated coffee

กาแฟไม่มีคาเฟอีน

G**ah**-F**ě** M**ø**-M**ee**-K**ah**-F**ě**-**ee**N

Tea

น้ำชา

N**ah**M-CH**ah**

Cream

ครีม

KR**ee**M

Sugar

น้ำตาล

N**ah**M-T**ah**N

Lemon

มะนาว

M**ah**-N**ow**

Milk

นม

NOM

Hot chocolate

ช็อคโกแล็ตร้อน

CHahK-GO-LềT RON

Juice

น้ำผลไม้

NahM PON-Lah-MI

Orange juice

น้ำส้ม

NahM SOM

Ice

น้ำแข็ง

NahM-KầNG

Ice water

น้ำเย็น

NahM-YềN

Bottled water

น้ำขวด

NahM-KooahT

AT THE BAR

Bartender
บาร์เทนเดอร์

B**ah**-T**e**N-D**o**

The wine list, please.
ขอเมนูไวน์

K**o** M**A**-N**oo** W**i**... (♦) KB**ah**P (♦) K**ah**

Cocktail
ค็อกเทล

K**ah**K-T**A**L

With ice
ใส่น้ำแข็ง

S**i** N**ah**M-K**a**NG

Without ice
ไม่ใส่น้ำแข็ง

M**i** S**i** N**ah**M-K**a**NG

With lemon
ใส่มะนาว

S**i** M**ah**-N**ow**

PHRASEMAKER

I would like a glass of…

ฉันอยากได้...แก้วนึง

CH(ah)N Y(ah)K D(I)...G(ĕ)(ow) N(ou)NG

- **champagne**

  แชมเปญ

  CH(ă)M P(A)N

- **beer**

  เบียร์

  B(EE)(ah)

- **wine**

  ไวน์

  W(I)

- **red wine**

  ไวน์แดง

  W(I) D(ă)NG

- **white wine**

  ไวน์ขาว

  W(I) K(ow)

(♂) KR(ah)P (♀) K(ah)

FAMILIAR FOODS

On the following pages you will
find lists of foods you are familiar
with, along with other information
such as basic utensils and preparation
instructions.

A polite way to get a waiter's or waitress's attention
is to say ฉันขอถามได้ไหม?, which means **May
I ask**, (pronunciation shown below) followed by
your request and thank you.

May I ask...

ฉันขอถามได้ไหม...

CH@N K© T@M D© M© W@...

Please bring me...

ขอ...หน่อย

K©...N@y

Thank you

ขอบคุณ

K@P KH@N

STARTERS

Appetizers

อาหารว่าง

@h-H@N-W@NG

Bread and butter

ขนมปังและเนย

K@h-N@M P@NG-L@ N@u-@E

Cheese

เนยแข็ง

N@u@E-K@NG

Fruit

ผลไม้

P@N-L@-M@

Salad

สลัด

S@h-L@hT

Soup

ซุป

S@P

MEAT

Bacon

เบค่อน

B**Ⓐ**-K**ⓐ**N

Beef

เนื้อวัว

N**ⓞⓤⓐⓗ** W**ⓞⓞⓐⓗ**

Beef steak

เสต็กเนื้อ

ST**Ⓐ**K N**ⓞⓞⓐⓗ**

Ham

แฮม

H**Ⓐ**M

Lamb

เนื้อแกะ

N**ⓞⓤⓐⓗ** G**ⓔ**

Pork

เนื้อหมู

N**ⓞⓤⓐⓗ** M**ⓞⓞ**

Veal

เนื้อลูกวัว

N**ⓞⓤⓐⓗ** L**ⓞⓞ**K W**ⓞⓞⓐⓗ**

POULTRY

Baked chicken

ไก่อบ

G① ⓞP

Broiled chicken

ไก่ย่าง

G① Y⊛NG

Fried chicken

ไก่ทอด

G① T⊘T

Duck

เป็ด

P⊕T

Goose

ห่าน

H⊛N

Turkey

ไก่งวง

G①-NY⊚⊛NG

SEAFOOD

Fish

ปลา

PL@ah@

Lobster

กุ้งมังกร

G@oo@NG-M@ah@NG-G@o@N

Oysters

หอยนางรม

H@oy@-N@ah@NG-B@o@M

Salmon

ปลาแซลมอน

PL@ah@-S@ah@L-M@o@N

Shrimp

กุ้ง

G@oo@NG

Trout	**Tuna**
ปลาเทร้าท์	ปลาทูน่า
PL@ah@-TB@ow@	PL@ah@-T@oo@-N@ah@

OTHER ENTREES

Sandwich
ขนมปังแซนด์วิช

K(ah) N(O)M P(ah)NG S(a)N-W(i)CH

Hot dog
ฮอทด็อก

H(ah)T D(a)(k)

Hamburger
แฮมเบอร์เกอร์

H(a)M-B(ur)-G(er)

French fries
เฟรนช์ฟราย

FR(e)N FR(i)

Pasta
พาสต้า

P(ah)S-T(ah)

Pizza
พิซซ่า

P(i)T-S(ah)

VEGETABLES

Carrots

แครอท

KE-BOT

Corn

ข้าวโพด

KOW-POT

Mushrooms

เห็ด

HeT

Onion

หัวหอม

HOOah-HOM

Potato

มันฝรั่ง

MaN-Fah-BaNG

Rice

ข้าว

KOW

Tomato

มะเขือเทศ

Mah-KOOah-TeT

FRUITS

Apple
แอ็ปเปิ้ล

ⓐP-PⓐⓝN

Banana
กล้วย

GLⓐⓐ

Grapes
องุ่น

ⓐN-GⓐⓝN

Lemon
มะนาว

Mⓐ-Nⓐ

Orange
ส้ม

SⓄM

Strawberry
สตรอเบอร์รี่

Sⓐ-Tⓐ-Bⓐ-Rⓐ

Watermelon
แตงโม

TⓐNG-MⓄ

DESSERT

Desserts

ของหวาน

KONG-WON

Apple pie

พายแอ็ปเบิ้ล

PI AP-PON

Cherry pie

พายเชอร์รี่

PI CHOU-REE

Pastries

ขนม

Kah-NOM

Candy

ลูกอม

LOK-OM

Ice cream

ไอติม

①-T①M

Ice cream cone

ไอติมโคน

①-T①M K①N

Chocolate

ช็อคโกแล็ต

CH⑱K-G①-L⑱T

Strawberry

สตรอเบอร์รี่

S⑱-T⑱-B⑪-R⑯

Vanilla

วนิลา

W⑱-N⑯-L⑱

CONDIMENTS

Butter

เนย

N**ou**EE

Ketchup

ซ๊อสมะเขือเทศ

S**ah**T-M**ah**-K**ou**ah-T**e**T

Mayonnaise

มายองเนส

M**ah**-Y**ah**NG-N**e**S

Mustard

มัสตาร์ด

M**ah**T-S**ah**-T**ah**T

Salt

เกลือ

GL**ou**ah

Pepper

พริกไท

PR**i**K-T**i**

Sugar

น้ำตาล

N**ah**M-T**ah**N

Vinegar

น้ำส้ม

N**ah**M-S**O**M-S**i**-CH**oo**

Oil

น้ำมัน

N**ah**M-M**ah**N

SETTINGS

A cup
ถ้วย

T@@

A glass
แก้ว

G@@

A spoon
ช้อน

CH@N

A fork
ส้อม

S@M

A knife
มีด

M@T

A plate
จาน

J@N

A napkin
ผ้าเช็ดปาก

P@ CH@T-P@K

HOW DO YOU WANT IT COOKED?

Baked

อบ

OP

Broiled

ย่าง

Y@NG

Steamed

นึ่ง

N@NG

Fried

ผัด / ทอด

P@T / TOT

Rare

ไม่สุก

MO-Sook

Medium	**Well done**
ปานกลาง	สุกมาก
P@N-GL@NG	Sook M@K

PROBLEMS

I didn't order this.

ฉันไม่ได้สั่งอันนี้

CH@N M@ D@ S@NG-@N-N€€

Is the bill correct?

บิลนี้ถูกต้องหรือเปล่า?

B@N N€€ T@K T@NG-B@-P@

Please bring me…

ขอ...หน่อย

K@...N@y

PRAISE

Thank you for the delicious meal.

ขอบคุณ อร่อยมาก

K@P KH@N @-B@y M@K KR@P (m)

K@P KH@N @-B@y M@K K@ (f)

GETTING AROUND

Getting around in a foreign country can be an adventure in itself! Taxi and bus drivers do not always speak English, so it is essential to be able to give simple directions. The words and phrases in this chapter will help you get where you're going.

- Aircon taxis offer the best way to get around. There is usually no problem finding a taxi as there are many.

- Have a map or the address you want to go to written down in Thai.

- Take a business card from your hotel to give to the taxi driver on your return.

- The Tuk-Tuk is a novel way to get around. This mode of transportation is basically a motorized rickshaw. It should be noted that it is very important to agree on the price of your trip before you embark.

- Skytrain compares to most cities mass transit systems. It is a good value and comfortable for traveling long distances. If you plan to use the skytrain regularly, you can purchase a convenient Skycard.

- Carry your ID with you at all times while in Thailand.

KEY WORDS

Airport

สนามบิน

S@h-N@M B@N

Bus station

สถานีขนส่ง

S@-T@-N@E K@N S@NG

Bus stop

ป้ายรถเมย์

P@-R@T-M@

Car rental agency

บริษัทรถเช่า

B@ R@E S@T R@T CH@

Subway station

สถานีรถไฟใต้ดิน

S@h-T@-N@E R@T-F@-T@-D@N

Taxi stand

ที่จอดรถแท็กซี่

T@ J@hT R@T T@K-S@

AIR TRAVEL

Airport

สนามบิน

S@h-N@hM-B①N

A one-way ticket, please.

ขอตั๋วเที่ยวเดียว

K◎　T⓪　TEE⓪w　DEE⓪w

A round trip ticket.

ตั๋วไปกลับ

T⓪⓪ah　P①　GL@hP

First class

ชั้นหนึ่ง

CH@hN　N⓪uNG

How much does it cost?

ราคาเท่าไหร่?

R@h-K@h　T⓪w-R①

PHRASEMAKER

I would like a seat…

ฉันต้องการที่นั่ง…

CH@N T@NG G@N T@ N@NG…

▶ **in first class**

ชั้นหนึ่ง

CH@N N@NG

▶ **next to the window**

ติดหน้าต่าง

T@T N@ T@NG

▶ **on the aisle**

ติดทางเดิน

T@T T@NG T@N

▶ **near the exit**

ใกล้ทางออก

GL@ T@NG @K

BY BUS

Bus

รถเมย์

BOT-MA

Where is the bus stop?

ป้ายรถเมย์อยู่ที่ไหน?

PI BOT-MA
Yoo TEE NO

Do you go to...?

คุณไป...ไหม?

KHOON PI...MO

What is the fare?

ค่าโดยสารราคาเท่าไหร่?

Kah Doy SahN Rah-Kah Tow-RI

How much does it cost?

ราคาเท่าไหร่?

Rah-Kah Tow-RI

(♀) KRahP (♂) Kah

PHRASEMAKER

Which bus goes to…

รถคันไหนไป...

ROT KaN NO PI…

▶ **the National Museum?**

พิพิธภัณฑ์แห่งชาติ?

PI PIT Tah PahN
HaNG CHOD

▶ **the Chatuchak Market?**

ตลาดจตุจักร?

Tah LahD Jah-Too JahK

▶ **Khao San Road?**

ถนนข้าวสาร?

TaN-NaN Kow SahN

▶ **the nearest beach?**

ชายหาดที่ใกล้ที่สุด?

CHI HahT TEE GLO
TEE SooD

BY CAR

Can you help me?

คุณช่วยฉันหน่อยได้ไหม?

KH⊙⊙N CH⊚⊚I CH⊚N
N⊚y D⊘ M⊙

My car won't start.

รถของฉันสตาร์ทไม่ติด

R⊙T K⊙NG CH⊚N
S⊚-T⊚T M⊘ T⊙T

Can you fix it?

คุณซ่อมได้ไหม?

KH⊙⊙N S⊚M D⊘ M⊙

What will it cost?

ราคาเท่าไหร่?

R⊚-K⊚ T⊚w-R⊘

How long will it take?

จะใช้เวลานานเท่าไหร่?

J⊚ CH⊘ W⊚-L⊚
N⊚N T⊚w-R⊘

PHRASEMAKER

Please check…

ช่วยเช็ค…

CHOOI CHEK… (♦) KRaP (♦) Kah

▶ **the battery**

หม้อแบตเตอรี่

MO BaT-Tou-REE

▶ **the brakes**

เบรค

BREK

▶ **the oil**

น้ำมัน

NahM MahN

▶ **the tires**

ยางรถ

YahNG ROT

▶ **the water**

น้ำ

NahM

SUBWAYS AND TRAINS

Where is the train station?

สถานีรถไฟอยู่ที่ไหน?

Sₐₕ-Tₐₕ-NEE ᏒOT-FI
YOO TEE NI

A one-way ticket, please.

ขอตั๋วเที่ยวเดียว

KO Tₒᵤ TEEₒw DEEₒw

A round trip ticket.

ตั๋วไปกลับ

Tₒᵤₐₕ PI GLₐₕP

First class

ชั้นหนึ่ง

CHₐₕN NₒᵤNG

Second class

ชั้นสอง

CHₐₕN SONG

What is the fare?

ค่าโดยสารราคาเท่าไหร่?

K@h D@y S@hN
R@h-K@h T@w-R①

Is this seat taken?

ที่นั่งนี้ถูกจองหรือยัง?

T@E-N@NG N@E
T@K J@hNG
R@w Y@uNG

Do I have to change trains?

ฉันต้องเปลี่ยนรถไฟไหม?

CH@N T@NG PL@E@N
R@T-F①-M①

Where are we?

เราอยู่ที่ไหน?

R@w Y@@ T@E N①

BY TAXI

Please call a taxi for me.
เรียกแท็กซี่ให้ฉันหน่อย

REE-ahK TaK-SEE HI
CHaN Noy

Are you available?
คุณว่างหรือเปล่า?

KHouN WaNG Rou PLow

I want to go…
ฉันต้องการไป…

CHaN TaNG GahN PI…

Stop here, please.
หยุดตรงนี

YoT TRONG NEE

Please wait.
กรุณารอตรงนี้

Gah-Rou-Nah RO TRONG NEE

How much does it cost?
ราคาเท่าไหร่?

Rah-Kah Tow-RI

(♦) KRahP (♦) Kah

PHRASEMAKER

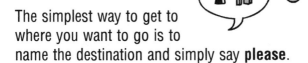

The simplest way to get to
where you want to go is to
name the destination and simply say **please**.

▶ **This address…**
ที่อยู่นี้…

T**EE**-Y**oo** (address) N**EE**…

▶ **This hotel…**
โรงแรมนี้…

R**O**NG-R**a**M (hotel name) N**EE**…

▶ **Airport…**
สนามบิน…

S**ah**-N**a**M B**i**N…

▶ **Subway station…**
สถานีรถไฟใต้ดิน…

S**ah**-T**a**-N**EE** R**O**T-F**i**-T**o**-D**i**N…

…please.
…กรุณา

…G**ah**-R**ou**-N**ah**

(♂) KR**ah**P (♀) K**ah**

SHOPPING

Whether you plan a major shopping spree or just need to purchase some basic necessities, the following information is useful.

- You can find duty-free shoping at Thailand Duty Free Shops Company in the World Trade Center.

- Thailand offers a variety of silks, silverware, pottery, jewlery, gemstones, as well as handicrafts.

- Tailored and off-the-rack clothing are readily available and inexpensive.

- It is a good idea to become familiar with pronunciation of numbers as bargaining is part of the tourist-customer-vendor relationship. Your knowledge could result in a cheaper price!

- Always remember to ask for receipts.

- It's best not to pack your purchases into your check-in luggage.

KEY WORDS

Credit card

บัตรเครดิต

B@hT KR@-D①T

Money

เงิน

NY⑩N

Receipt

ใบเสร็จ

B①-S@T

Sale

ลดราคา

L①T-R@h-K@h

Store

ร้านค้า

R@hN-K@h

Traveler's checks

เช็คเดินทาง

CH@K D⑩N-T@hNG

USEFUL PHRASES

Do you sell…?

คุณขาย…ไหม?

KHOON KOY…MOY

Do you have…?

คุณมี…ไหม?

KHOON MEE…MOY

I want to buy.

ฉันต้องการซื้อ

CHAN DONG GahN SOO

How much?

เท่าไหร่?

TOW-ROY

When are the shops open?

ร้านเปิดกี่โมง?

RahN POOD GEE MONG

No, thank you.

ไม่ ขอบคุณ

M**Ⓘ** K**ⓐ**P K**ʰⓞⓞ**N

I´m just looking.

ดูเฉยเฉย

D**ⓞⓞ** CH**ⓞⓔⓔ** CH**ⓞⓔⓔ**

Is it very expensive?

แพงไปไหม?

P**ⓐ**NG P**Ⓘ** M**Ⓘ**

Can't you give me a discount?

ลดราคาหน่อยได้ไหม?

L**ⓞ**D R**ⓐ**h K**ⓐ**h N**ⓞ**y
D**Ⓘ** M**Ⓘ**

I'll take it.

ฉันจะเอาอันนี้

CH**ⓐ**N J**ⓐ**h-**ⓞⓦ** **ⓐ**hN N**ⓔⓔ**

I'd like a receipt, please.

ขอใบเสร็จด้วย

K**Ⓘ** B**Ⓘ** S**ⓔ**T D**ⓞⓦⒾ**

SHOPS AND SERVICES

Bakery

ขนมปัง

K@h-N@M-P@NG

Bank	**Hair salon**
ธนาคาร	ร้านทำผม
T@-N@h-K@N	R@N-T@M-P@M

Jewelry store

ร้านขายเครื่องประดับ

R@N-K①-KR@@NG-PR@h-D@P

Bookstore

ร้านขายหนังสือ

R@N-K① N@NG-S@

Camera shop

ร้านขายกล้องถ่ายรูป

R@N-K① GL@NG-T①-R@P

Pharmacy

ร้านขายยา

R@N-K①-Y@h

SHOPPING LIST

On the following pages you will find some common items you may need to purchase on your trip.

Aspirin

ยาแอสไพริน

Y(ah)-(a)S-P(i)-R(i)N

Cigarettes

บุหรี่

B(oo)-R(EE)

Deodorant

ยาดับกลิ่นตัว

Y(ah)-D(ah)P-GL(i)N-T(oo)(ah)

Dress

ชุดกระโปรง

CH(oo)T-GR(ah)-PR(o)NG

Film (camera)

ฟิล์ม

F(i)M

Perfume

น้ำหอม

N@M-H@M

Razor blades

ใบมีดโกน

B@ M@T G@N

Shampoo

ยาสระผม

Y@-S@-P@M

Shaving cream

ครีมโกนหนวด

KR@M G@N-N@@@T

Shirt

เสื้อเชิ๊ต

S@@@-SH@T

Sunglasses

แว่นกันแดด

W@N-G@N-D@T

Suntan oil

ครีมกันแดด

KREEM GahN DaT

Toothbrush

แปรงสีฟัน

PRahNG-SEE-FahN

Toothpaste

ยาสีฟัน

Yah-SEE-FahN

Water (bottled)

น้ำขวด

NahM KooahT

Water (mineral)

น้ำแร่

NahM Rae

ESSENTIAL SERVICES

THE BANK

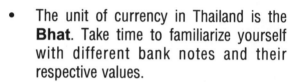

As a traveler in a foreign country your primary contact with banks will be to exchange money.

- The unit of currency in Thailand is the **Bhat**. Take time to familiarize yourself with different bank notes and their respective values.

- Have your passport handy when changing money. Cash or traveler's checks can be exchanged for Thai currency at banks or exchange bureaus.

- Do not display money in public.

- ATMs offer easy and convenient way to change money; however, you should check to see what fee your bank will charge before using this method.

- Most major credit cards are accepted; however, it is a good idea to check with your bank to see if your credit card is accepted.

KEY WORDS

Bank

ธนาคาร

T⒜-N⒜-K⒜N

Exchange office

ที่แลกเงินต่างประเทศ

T⒠ L⒜G NY⒪N T⒜NG PR⒜-T⒠T

Money

เงิน

NY⒪N

Money order

ใบสั่งจ่ายเงิน

B⒤ S⒜NG J⒤ NY⒪N

Traveler's check

เช็คเดินทาง

CH⒠K D⒪N T⒜NG

USEFUL PHRASES

Where is the bank?

ธนาคารอยู่ที่ไหน?

T⒜-N⒜-K⒜N YOO T⒠ N◯

What time does the bank open?

ธนาคารเปิดกี่โมง?

T⒜-N⒜-K⒜N P⒪D G⒠ M◯NG

Where is the exchange office?

...ที่แลกเงินต่างประเทศอยู่ที่ไหน?

T⒠ L⒜G NY⒪N T⒜NG
P⒭-T⒠T YOO T⒠ N◯

What time does the exchange office open?

ที่แลกเงินต่างประเทศเปิดกี่โมง?

T⒠ L⒜G NY⒪N T⒜NG
P⒭-T⒠T P⒪D G⒠ M◯NG

Can I change dollars here?

ฉันแลกเงิน ยู เอส ดอลลาร์ที่นี่ได้ไหม?

CH⒜N L⒜G NY⒪N
U.S. D⒜-L⒜R
T⒠-N⒠ D◯ M◯

(♦) KB⒭P (♦) K⒜h

What is the exchange rate?

อัตราแลกเปลี่ยนเท่าไหร่?

ahT-TRah LͻG
PLEEN TOW-RͽI

I would like large bills.

ฉันอยากได้แบ๊งค์ใหญ่

CHͻN YahK Dͻ BㆍNG Yͽl

I would like small bills.

ฉันอยากได้แบ๊งค์เล็ก

CHͻN YahK Dͻ BㆍNG LĕK

I need change.

ฉันต้องการเงินเหรียญ

CHͻN TONG GahN NYOUN RͽEN

Do you have an ATM?

มีตู้เอทีเอ็มไหม?

MEE TOW ATM Mͽl

POST OFFICE

If you are planning on sending letters and postcards, be sure to send them early so that you don't arrive home before they do.

KEY WORDS

Air mail

ไปรษณีย์

PRO-Sah-NEE

Letter

จดหมาย

JOT-MO

Post office

ที่ทำการไปรษณีย์

TEE-TahM-GahN-PRO-Sah-NEE

Postcard

ไปรษณียบัตร

PRO-Sah-NEE-Yah-BuhT

Stamp

แสตมป์

Sah-TahM

USEFUL PHRASES

Where is the post office?

ที่ทำการไปรษณีย์อยู่ที่ไหน?

TEE TahM Gahn PROI-Sah-NEE
Yoo TEE NOI

What time does the post office open?

ที่ทำการไปรษณีย์เปิดกี่โมง?

TEE-TahM Gahn PROI-Sah-NEE
PooD GEE MONG

I need...

ฉันต้องการ...

CHon TONG Gahn

▶ **stamps**

แสตมป์

Sah-TâM

▶ **an envelope**

ซองจดหมาย

SONG JoT-MOI

TELEPHONE

Placing phone calls in Thailand can
be a test of will and stamina! Besides
the obvious language barriers, service
can vary greatly from one town to the
next.

- The easiest way to make international
  calls is the availability of calling services
  located in Internet cafes and guest houses
  in tourist areas.

- Calls in Thailand can also be made by
  purchasing a SIM card and placing it in
  your phone.

- Purchasing a cheap phone with prepaid
  calling card is also an option easy to obtain
  and have service in about an hour.

- Internet cafes offer phone services via
  computer and Internet connections.

KEY WORDS

Information

ข้อมูล

KO-MooN

Long distance

ทางไกล

TahNG GLI

Operator

พนักงานรับโทรศัพท์

Pah-NahK-NYahN-TO-Rah-SahP

Phone book

สมุดโทรศัพท์

Sah-MooT TO-RuhB-SahP

Public telephone

โทรศัพท์สาธารณะ

TO-Rah-SahP Sah-Tah-Rah-Nah

Telephone

โทรศัพท์

TO-Rah-SahP

USEFUL PHRASES

Where is the telephone?

โทรศัพท์อยู่ที่ไหน?

TO-Rah-SahP YOO TEE NO

Where is the public telephone?

โทรศัพท์สาธารณะอยู่ที่ไหน?

TO-Rah-SahP Sah-Tah-Rah-Nah
YOO TEE NO

May I use your telephone?

ฉันขอใช้โทรศัพท์ของคุณได้ไหม?

CHaN KO CHO
TO-Rah-SahP KONG
KHOON DO MO

I don't speak Thai.

ฉันพูดภาษาไทยไม่ได้

CHaN POT Pah-Sah
TO MO DO

(♂) KRahP   (♀) Kah

I want to call this number…

ฉันต้องการโทรเบอร์นี้...

CH⬚N T⬚NG G⬚N TO B⬚ N⬚…
(♂) KR⬚P (♀) K⬚

1	2	3
หนึ่ง	สอง	สาม
N⬚NG	S⬚NG	S⬚M

4	5	6
สี่	ห้า	หก
S⬚	H⬚	H⬚K

7	8	9
เจ็ด	แปด	เก้า
J⬚T	P⬚T	G⬚

★	0	#
	ศูนย์	
	S⬚N	

SIGHTSEEING AND ENTERTAINMENT

Bangkok (Krung Thep) is the capital of Thailand. It is home to several temples, historical and cultural sites.

Respect is of utmost importance in Thai culture and should be considered a priority. Dressing conservatively and removing shoes when entering homes and sacred buildings is customary.

Additionally, pointing feet in the direction or making a kicking motion in the direction of anyone or anything is considered disrepectful.

The heart of the city of Bangkok and the area where most tourists stay is on the east side of the Chao Phraya river. The Chao Phraya river cuts Bangkok in half creating several waterways for tourists to enjoy touring and sightseeing. You can find river express and canal boats at bargain prices.

Wat Phra Kaew, Temple of the Emerald Buddha, is a sacred symbol of Rattanakosin and is located on the grounds of the Grand Palace in central Bangkok. All temples are inspired by Buddhism, and this has a strong influence on the people of Thailand. Its effect is seen everywhere in Thailand in its people, architecture, arts, and crafts.

KEY WORDS

Admission
ค่าเข้า

Kah-Kow

Map
แผนที่

PaN-Tee

Reservation
การจอง

GahN-JONG

Ticket
ตั๋ว

Tooah

Tour
ทัวร์

Tooah

Tour guide
ไกด์ทัวร์

GI Tooah

USEFUL PHRASES

Where is the tourist agency?
สำนักงานท่องเที่ยวอยู่ที่ไหน?

S**ⓐ**M N**ⓐ**K NY**ⓐ**N T**ⓐ**NG
T**ⓔⓔ**ow Y**ⓞⓞ** T**ⓔⓔ** N**ⓞ** (♀) KR**ⓐ**P (♂) K**ⓐ**h

Where do I buy a ticket?
ฉันต้องซื้อตั๋วที่ไหน?

CH**ⓐ**N <u>T</u>**ⓞ**NG S**ⓞⓤ** <u>T</u>**ⓞⓞ**ah T**ⓔⓔ** N**ⓞ**

How much?
เท่าไหร่?

T**ⓞⓦ** R**ⓞ**

How long?
นานเท่าไหร่?

N**ⓐ**N T**ⓞⓦ**-R**ⓞ**

When?
เมื่อไหร่?

M**ⓞⓦ**ah-R**ⓞ**

Where?
ที่ไหน?

T**ⓔⓔ**-N**ⓞ**

Do I need reservations?

ฉันต้องจองไหม?

CHΑN TΑNG
JΟNG MΟ (♂) KRΑP (♀) KΑh

Does the guide speak English?

ไกด์พูดภาษาอังกฤษหรือเปล่า?

GΙ POOT PΑh-SΑh
ΑNG-GRΙT RΟ PLOW

How much do children pay?

เด็กต้องจ่ายราคาเท่าไหร่?

DΕK TΑNG JΙ
RΑh-KΑh TOW RΙ

I need your help.

ฉันต้องการความช่วยเหลือจากคุณ

CHΑN TΑNG GΑRN KWΑM
CHOOI LOOΑ JΑK KHΟN

Thank you.

ขอบคุณ

KΑP KHOON

PHRASEMAKER

I'm looking for…

ฉันกำลังมองหา…

CH@N G@M-L@NG M@NG H@…

▶ **the Chatuchak Market**

ตลาดจตุจักร

T̲ah L@hD J@h-T̲oo J@hK

This is a very popular market in Bangkok.

▶ **the Emerald Temple**

วัดพระแกว

W@hD PR@h G@ow

The temple of the Emerald Buddha is located on the
grounds of the Grand Palace.

▶ **Wat Arun on Chaophraya River**

วัดอรุณราชวาราม

W@hD @h-R@@N

R@h-CH@h-W@h-R@h-R@hM

▶ **Khao San Road**

ถนนข้าวสาร

T@h-N@N-K@wS@hN

Khao San Road is a popular destination and the definition of
"Party-On." It is a happy place to get acclimated to Thai night
life, delicious Thai restaurant fare, bars, pubs, and fun day and
night shopping.

▶ **a swimming pool**

สระว่ายน้ำ

S@h WO N@hM

▶ **a movie theater**

โรงหนัง

R@NG N@NG

▶ **a health club**

ชมรมสุขภาพ

CH@M R@M
S@-K@h-P@hP

▶ **a tennis court**

สนามเทนนิส

S@h-N@M T@N-N@T

▶ **a golf course**

สนามกอล์ฟ

S@h-N@M G@P

HEALTH

Hopefully you will not need medical attention on your trip. If you do, it is important to communicate basic information regarding your condition.

- Check with your insurance company before leaving home to find out if you are covered in a foreign country. You may want to purchase traveler's insurance before leaving home.

- If you take prescription medicine, carry your prescription with you. Have your prescriptions translated into Thai characters before you leave home.

- Take a small first-aid kit with you. You may want to include basic cold and anti-diarrhea medications. However, you should be able to find most items like aspirin locally.

- In Thailand you cannot drink water from the tap as you may be used to at home. Always drink bottled water.

- Bangkok offers excellent health care and is home to the world-renowned Bumrungrad hospital.

- Pharmacies are widely located and some are open late into the night.

KEY WORDS

Ambulance

รถพยาบาล

ROT P@h-Y@h-B@hN

Dentist

หมอฟัน

MO-F@hN

Doctor

หมอ

MO

Emergency

เหตุฉุกเฉิน

H@T-CH@K-CH@N

Hospital

โรงพยาบาล

RONG P@h-Y@h-B@hN

Prescription

ใบสั่งยา

B@-S@hNG-Y@h

USEFUL PHRASES

I am sick.

ฉันไม่สบาย

CH**ⓐ**N M**ⓘ**
S**ⓐ**h-B**ⓘ**

I need a doctor.

ฉันต้องการไปหาหมอ

CH**ⓐ**N T**ⓐ**NG G**ⓐ**N
P**ⓘ** H**ⓐ**h M**ⓞ**

It's an emergency!

มันเป็นเหตุฉุกเฉิน!

M**ⓤ**N P**ⓔ**N H**ⓔ**T CH**ⓞⓞ**K-CH**ⓤ**N

Where is the nearest hospital?

โรงพยาบาลที่ใกล้ที่สุดอยู่ที่ไหน?

R**ⓞ**NG P**ⓐ**h-Y**ⓐ**h-B**ⓐ**N T**ⓔⓔ**
GL**ⓘ** T**ⓔⓔ** S**ⓞⓞ**T Y**ⓞⓞ** T**ⓔⓔ** N**ⓘ**

Call an ambulance!

ตามรถพยาบาล!

T**ⓐ**M R**ⓞ**T P**ⓐ**h-Y**ⓐ**h-B**ⓐ**N

(♂ KR**ⓐ**P ♀ K**ⓐ**)

I'm allergic to…

ฉันแพ้…

CHⓐN Pâ…

I'm pregnant.

ฉันตั้งครรภ์

CHⓐN TⓤNG KⓤhN

I'm diabetic.

ฉันเป็นเบาหวาน

CHⓐN Pē̆N Bⓞⓦ WⓐN

I have a heart condition.

ฉันเป็นโรคหัวใจ

CHⓐN Pē̆N RⓞⓀ Hⓞⓞⓐh-JⒾ

I have high blood pressure.

ฉันเป็นความดันโลหิตสูง

CHⓐN Pē̆N KWⓐhM DⓐhN
LⓄ HⒾT Sⓐ̃NG

I have low blood pressure.

ฉันเป็นความดันโลหิตต่ำ

CHⓐN Pē̆N KWⓐhM DⓐhN
LⓄ HⒾT TⓐhM

PHRASEMAKER

I need…

ฉันต้องการ...

CH**ô**N T**O**NG G**ah**N... (♦ KR**ah**P ♦ K**ah**)

▸ **a doctor**

หมอ

M**O**

▸ **a dentist**

หมอฟัน

M**O**-F**uh**N

▸ **a nurse**

พยาบาล

P**ah**-Y**ah**-B**ah**N

▸ **an optician**

หมอตา

M**O**-T**ah**

▸ **a pharmacist**

เภสัชกร

P**A**-S**ah**T-CH**ah**-G**O**N

PHRASEMAKER
(AT THE PHARMACY)

Do you have…

คุณมี....ไหม

KʰⓄN MⒺⒺ...MⓋ (♂ KRⓐP   ♂ Kⓐ)

▸ **aspirin?**

ยาแอสไพริน

Yⓐ-ⓐS-PⒾ-RⓄN

▸ **Band-Aids?**

พลาสเตอร์ยา

PLⓐD-Sⓐ-TⓊ Yⓐ

▸ **cough syrup?**

ยาน้ำแก้ไอ

Yⓐ-NⓐM-Gⓐ-Ⓘ

▸ **ear drops?**

ยาหยอดหู

Yⓐ-YⓄD-HⓄⓄ

▸ **eye drops?**

ยาหยอดตา

Yⓐ-YⓄD-Tⓐ

BUSINESS TRAVEL

It is important to show appreciation and interest in another person's language and culture, particularly when doing business. A few well-pronounced phrases can make a great impression.

- The wai greeting is the standard greeting in Thailand. It is accomplished by putting hands together, bringing them up to the chest while slightly bowing and just touching the nose with your closed palms. It is a sign of respect shown to those who are older or of higher social status.

- It is wise to show tolerance, acceptance, and respect in order to save face while doing business with Thais.

- Exchanging business cards is very important, so be sure to bring a good supply with you. It is a good idea to have your business card printed in Thai characters.

- Business dress is conservative for both men and women.

- Body language is extremely important whether conducting business or in everyday interaction with Thais.

- Do not reach over the head of your Thai counterpart for something as this is disrespectful.

KEY WORDS

Appointment

การนัด

G@N-N@T

Business card

นามบัตร

N@M-B@T

Meeting

การประชุม

G@N PR@-CH@M

Marketing

การตลาด

G@N-T@-L@D

Office

สำนักงาน

S@M-N@K NY@N

Presentation

การนำเสนอ

G@N N@M
S@-N@

Telephone

โทรศัพท์

T@-R@-S@P

USEFUL PHRASES

I have an appointment.

ฉันมีนัด

CHⓐN MⒺE NⓊT

My name is…(your name).

ฉันชื่อ…

CHⓐN CHⓄO…(your name)

Pleased to meet you.

ยินดีที่ได้พบคุณ

YⒾN DⒺE TⒺ DⓄ PⓄP KHⓄO N

Here is my card.

นี่คือนามบัตรของฉัน

NⒺE KⓄO NⓐM BⓊT
KⓄNG CHⓐN

Can we get an interpreter?

ฉันขอล่ามได้ไหม?

CHⓐN KⓄ
LⓐM DⓄ MⓄ

(♦) KRⓐP (♦) Kⓐ

Can you write your address for me?

คุณช่วยเขียนที่อยู่ของคุณให้ฉันได้ไหม?

KʰOON CHOOI KEEahN TEE YOO
KONG KʰOON HI CHaN DO MO

Can you write your phone number?

คุณช่วยเขียนเบอร์โทรศัพท์ของคุณให้ฉันได้ไหม?

KʰOON CHOOI KEEahN BUr
TO-Rah-Sah P KONG KʰOON HI
CHaN DO MO

This is my phone number.

นี่คือเบอร์โทรศัพท์ของฉัน

NEE KOO BUr
TO-Rah-SahP KONG CHaN

His / Her name is…

เขาชื่อ…

KOW CHOO…

Good-bye.

ลาก่อน

Lah-GON

(♦) KRahP (♦) Kah

PHRASEMAKER

I need…
ฉันต้องการ...

CH@N T⊙NG G@N... (♦) KR@P (♦) K@h

▶ **a computer**
คอมพิวเตอร์

KⓄM-Pⓔⓦ-Tⓞⓤ

▶ **a copy machine**
เครื่องถ่ายเอกสาร

KRⓌ@NG-T①-ⒺⒺK-G@h-S@N

▶ **a conference room**
ห้องประชุม
HⓄNG PR@-CHⓄM

▶ **a fax or fax machine**
เครื่องแฟกซ์

KRⓌ@NG-F@K

▶ **an interpreter**
ล่าม

L@M

▶ **a lawyer**

ทนายความ

T@h-N①-KW@hM

▶ **a notary**

พนักงานทะเบียน

P@h-N@hK-NY@hN-T@h-B㋐㋐㋒N

▶ **a pen**

ปากกา

P@hK-G@h

▶ **stamps**

แสตมป์

S@h-T@M

▶ **stationery**

อุปกรณ์สำนักงาน

㋦P-P@h-G①N-S@M-N@hK-NY@hN

▶ **paper**

กระดาษ

GR@h-D@hT

GENERAL INFORMATION

SEASONS

Spring

ฤดูใบไม้ผลิ

R⁰⁰-D⁰⁰-BⒾ-M①-PLⓘ

Summer

ฤดูร้อน

R⁰⁰-D⁰⁰-R⓪N

Autumn

ฤดูใบไม้ร่วง

R⁰⁰-D⁰⁰-BⒾ-M①-R⓪⓪ahNG

Winter

ฤดูหนาว

R⁰⁰-D⁰⁰-N⓪ⓌⓌ

THE DAYS

Monday
วันจันทร์

W@N-J@N

Tuesday
วันอังคาร

W@N-@NG-K@N

Wednesday
วันพุธ

W@N-P@T

Thursday
วันพฤหัสบดี

W@N-P@-R@-H@T-S@-B@-D@

Friday
วันศุกร์

W@N-S@K

Saturday
วันเสาร์

W@N-S@

Sunday
วันอาทิตย์

W@N-@-T@T

THE MONTHS

January

เดือนมกราคม

D⍟N M⍟-G⍟-R⍟-KOM

February

เดือนกุมภาพันธ์

D⍟N GOOM-P⍟-P⍟N

March

เดือนมีนาคม

D⍟N MEE-N⍟-KOM

April

เดือนเมษายน

D⍟N M⍟-S⍟-YON

May

เดือนพฤษภาคม

D⍟N PR⍟T-S⍟-P⍟-KOM

June

เดือนมิถุนายน

D⍟N M⍟-T⍟-N⍟-YON

July

เดือนกรกฎาคม

D**ou**ahN G**ah**-R**ah**-G**ah**-D**ah**-K**O**M

August

เดือนสิงหาคม

D**ou**ahN S**O**NG-H**a**-K**O**M

September

เดือนกันยายน

D**ou**ahN G**ah**N-Y**ah**-Y**O**N

October

เดือนตุลาคม

D**ou**ahN T**oo**-L**ah**-K**O**M

November

เดือนพฤศจิกายน

D**ou**ahN PR**ou**T-S**ah**-J**i**-G**ah**-Y**O**N

December

เดือนธันวาคม

D**ou**ahN T**ah**N-W**ah**-K**O**M

COLORS

Black
สีดำ
SEE-DahM

White
สีขาว
SEE-Kow

Blue (light)
สีฟ้า
SEE-Fah

Brown
สีน้ำตาล
SEE-NahM-TahN

Gray
สีเทา
SEE-Tow

Gold
สีทอง
SEE-TONG

Orange
สีส้ม
SEE-SOM

Yellow
สีเหลือง
SEE-LooahNG

Red
สีแดง
SEE-DaNG

Green
สีเขียว
SEE-KEEow

Pink
สีชมพู
SEE-CHOM-Poo

Purple
สีม่วง
SEE-MooahNG

NUMBERS

0	**1**
ศูนย์	หนึ่ง
S⊙N	N⊙NG
2	**3**
สอง	สาม
S⊙NG	S⊙M
4	**5**
สี่	ห้า
S⊙	H⊙
6	**7**
หก	เจ็ด
H⊙K	J⊙T
8	**9**
แปด	เก้า
P⊙T	G⊙
10	**11**
สิบ	สิบเอ็ด
S⊙P	S⊙P-⊙T

12

สิบสอง

SiP-SONG

13

สิบสาม

SiP-SaM

14

สิบสี่

SiP-SEE

15

สิบห้า

SiP-Hah

16

สิบหก

SiP-HOK

17

สิบเจ็ด

SiP-JeT

18

สิบแปด

SiP-PaT

19

สิบเก้า

SiP-GOW

20

ยี่สิบ

YEE-SiP

30

สามสิบ

SaM-SiP

40

สี่สิบ

SEE-SiP

50

ห้าสิบ

Hah-SiP

60

หกสิบ

HOK-SiP

70

เจ็ดสิบ

JeT-SiP

80

แปดสิบ

P_@T-S(i)P

90

เก้าสิบ

G(@w)-S(i)P

100

หนึ่งร้อย

N(@u)NG-B(@y)

1,000
หนึ่งพัน

N(@u)NG-P(@h)N

1,000,000
หนึ่งล้าน

N(@u)NG-L(@h)N

DICTIONARY

Each English entry is followed
by standard Thai characters and
then the EPLS Vowel Symbol
System of pronunciation.

The Thai language is quite concise and doesn't
use as many words to convey a thought or idea
as in English. Additionally, pronouns are left out
of sentences but understood based on context.
There are no equivalents for the English articles
a, an, or the.

Words in this book and dictionary are not translated
literally. For example the literal translation for the
English words "**yes**" and "**no**" are "**want**" and "**not
want**" respectively.

ABSOLUTE RULE: In Thai it is important to make
a conscious effort to add ครับ KR@P คะ K@ after
a phrase. Khrap is always spoken by a male and
Kha is spoken by female. This makes the sentence
or phrase less abrupt and is very important to the
language without question.

Symbols used in this book:

(m) Masculine

(f) Feminine

(♦) Male speaking

(♦) Female speaking

A

a lot มาก M@K

above ข้างบน K@NG-B@N

accident อุบัติเหตุ @-B@T-T@-H@T

accommodation ที่พัก T@-P@K

account บัญชี B@N-CH@

address ที่อยู่ T@-Y@

admission ค่าเข้า K@-K@

afraid (to be) กลัว GL@@

afternoon ตอนบ่าย T@N-B@

air-conditioning เครื่องปรับอากาศ
  KR@NG PR@P-@-G@D

airline สายการบิน S@-G@N-B@N

airport สนามบิน S@-N@M-B@N

aisle ทางเดิน T@NG-D@N

all ทั้งหมด T@NG-M@T

almost เกือบ G@@P

alone เดียว D@@

also ด้วย D@@

always (forever and ever) ตลอดไป
  T@-L@T P@

ambulance รถพยาบาล R@T-P@-Y@-B@N

American คนอเมริกัน KON-ah-ME-RI-GahN

and และ Lä

another (another one of the same) อีก EEK

apartment อพาร์ทเมนท์ ah-PahT-MEN

apple แอ็ปเปิ้ล äP-PaN

appointment การนัด GahN-NahT

April เดือนเมษายน DouahN ME-Sa-YON

arrival ขาเข้า Ka-Kow

ashtray ที่เขี่ยบุหรี่ TEE-KEE-ah Boo-REE

aspirin ยาแอสไพริน Yah-äS-PI-RIN

August เดือนสิงหาคม DouahN SONG-Ha-KOM

Australia ประเทศออสเตรเลีย
    PRah-TE-TO-Sah-TRE-LEEah

Australian คนออสเตรเลีย
    KO-NO-Sah-TRE-LEEah

automated teller machine ตู้เอทีเอ็ม TOO ATM

autumn ฤดูใบไม้ร่วง
    Roo-Doo-BI-MI-Roo-ahNG

avenue ถนน Tah-NON

awful แย่ Yä

B

baby ทารก Tah-ROK

babysitter พี่เลี้ยงเด็ก PEE-LEEahNG-DehK

bacon เบค่อน BA-KawN

bad เลว LEou

bag ถุง TooNG

baggage กระเป๋า GBahP-Pow

bakery ร้านขายขนมปัง
    BAN-KO-Kah-NOM-PahNG

banana กล้วย GLooA

Band-Aid พลาสเตอร์ PLah-Sah-Tou

bank ธนาคาร Tah-Nah-KahN

barber ช่างตัดผม CHahNG-TahT-POM

bartender บาร์เทนเดอร์ Bah-TEN-Dou

bath อ่างน้ำ ahNG-NahM

bathing suit ชุดว่ายน้ำ CHooT WOA NahM

bathroom ห้องน้ำ HONG-NahM

battery แบตเตอรี่ BahT-Tou-BEE

beach ชายหาด CHOI-HahT

beautiful สวย SOEE

beauty salon ร้านเสริมสวย BahN SowM SOEE

bed เตียง DEEahNG

beef เนื้อวัว Nouah Wooah

beer เบียร์　Bⓔⓔaⓗ

big ใหญ่　Yⓘ

bill บิล　BⓘN

black สีดำ　Sⓔⓔ-DⓐⓗM

blanket ผ้าห่ม　Pⓐⓨ-HⓞⓜM

blue สีฟ้า　Sⓔⓔ-Fⓐⓗ

boat เรือ　Bⓞⓤaⓗ

book หนังสือ　NⓐNG-Sⓞⓤ

bookshop ร้ายขายหนังสือ　BⓐⓗN-Kⓞ　NⓐNG-Sⓞⓤ

border (country)　ชายแดน　CHⓘ-DⓐⓗN

boy เด็กชาย　DⓔK-CHⓘ

bracelet กำไลมือ　GⓐⓗM-Lⓘ　Mⓞⓤ

brakes เบรค　BBⓔK

bread ขนมปัง　Kⓐⓗ-NⓞM-PⓐⓗNG

breakfast อาหารเช้า　ⓐⓗ-HⓐⓗN-CHⓞⓦ

brother พี่ชาย　Pⓔⓔ　CHⓘ (older)
　　　　น้องชาย　NⓞNG　CHⓘ (younger)

brown สีน้ำตาล　Sⓔⓔ-NⓐⓗM-TⓐⓗN

brush (hair)　แปรง　PBⓐNG

building ตึก　TⓞⓤK

bus (city)　รถเมย์　BⓞT-MⓔB

bus station สถานีขนส่ง
  S(ah)-TH(a)-N(EE) K(O)N-S(o)NG

bus stop ป้ายรถเมย์ P(Z)-B(o)T-M(E)B

business ธุรกิจ T(oo)-B(ah)-G(i)T

butter เนย N(ou)(EE)

buy (to) ซื้อ S(ou)

C

cafe ร้านกาแฟ B(ah)N-G(ah)-F(e)

call (to) เรียก B(E)(ah)K

camera กล้องถ่ายรูป GL(O)NG-T(I)-B(oo)P

Canada ประเทศแคนาดา PB(ah)-T(E)T K(a)-N(ah)-D(ah)

Canadian คนแคนาดา K(O)N K(a)-N(ah)-D(ah)

candy ลูกอม L(oo)K-(O)M

car รถยนต์ B(O)T-Y(O)N

carrot แครอท K(a)-B(o)T

castle ปราสาท PB(ah)-S(ah)T

cathedral โบสถ์ B(o)T

celebration การฉลอง G(ah)N CH(ah)-L(O)NG

cereal (cold) ซีเรียล S(EE)-B(e)-(ah)N

chair เก้าอี้ G(ou)(EE)

champagne แชมเป็ญ CH(a)M-P(a)N

change (money) แลก   L**@**K

change (to) เปลี่ยนแปลง   PL**EE@**N   PL**@**NG

cheap ถูก   T**oo**K

check (restaurant bill) เช็คบิล   CH**E**K-B**i**N

cheese เนยแข็ง   N**ouE**-K**@**NG

chicken ไก่   G**i**

child เด็ก   D**e**K

chocolate ช็อกโกแล็ต   CH**@**K-G**O**-L**e**T

church โบสถ์   B**o**T

cigar บุหรี่ซิการ์   B**oo**-B**EE**   S**i**-G**@**

cigarette บุหรี่   B**oo**-B**EE**

city เมือง   M**ouah**NG

clean สะอาด   S**ah@h**T

clock นาฬิกา   N**ah**-L**EE**-G**ah**

closed ปิดแล้ว   P**EE**T-L**@h**ou

clothing เสื้อผ้า   S**uah**-P**@**

cocktail ค็อกเทล   K**@h**K-T**@**L

coffee กาแฟ   G**ah**-F**e**

cold (temperature) หนาว   N**ow**

comb หวี   W**EE**

computer คอมพิวเตอร์   K**O**M-P**ew**-T**@**

conference การประชุม GAHN-PRAH-CHOOM

congratulations ขอแสดงความยินดี
KO-SAH-DANG-KWAHM-YIN-DEE

copy machine เครื่องถ่ายเอกสาร
KRUAHNG TIE-EEK-GAH-SAHN

corn ข้าวโพด KOW-POT

cough syrup ยาน้ำแก้ไอ YAH-NAHM-GOI

cover charge ค่าผ่านประตู KOW-PAHN-PAH-TOO

crab ปู POO

credit card บัตรเครดิต BAHT KRAY-DIT

cup ถ้วย TOOAY

customs ศุลกากร SOON-LAH-GAH-GON

D

dance (to) เต้นรำ TEN-BAHM

dangerous อันตราย AHN-TAH-BIE

day วัน WAHN

December เดือนธันวาคม DUAHN-TAHN-WAH-KOM

delicious อร่อย AH-ROY

dentist หมอฟัน MO-FUHN

deodorant ยาดับกลิ่นตัว
YAH-DAHP-GLEEN-TOOAH

department store ห้างสรรพสินค้า
  HONG SaP-Pah-SON-Kah

departure ขาออก KaOK

dessert ของหวาน KONG-WaN

diabetic โรคเบาหวาน BOK-Bow-WaN

diarrhea ท้องเสีย TONG SEEah

dictionary พจนานุกรม POT-Jah-Nah-Noo-GROM

dining room ห้องทานอาหาร
  HONG TaN-ah-HaN

dinner อาหารเย็น ah-HaN-YeN

direction ทิศทาง TOT-TaNG

dirty สกปรก SOK-Gah-PROK

disabled พิการ PI-GaN

discount ลดราคาสินค้า
  LOT-Bah-Kah-SON-Kah

distance ระยะทาง Bah-Yah-TaNG

dizziness เวียนหัว WEEeN-Hooa

doctor หมอ MO

dollar ดอลลาร์ DON-Lw

down ลง LONG

drink (to) เครื่องดื่ม KBwahNG-DwM

dry แห้ง HaNG

duck　เป็ด　P̲ĕT

E

ear　หู　Hoo

ear drops　ยาหยอดหู　Yah-YoD-Hoo

early　เช้า　CHow

east　ทิศตะวันออก　T̲EET-T̲ah-WahN-oK

easy　ง่าย　NYI

eat (to)　ทาน / กิน　TahN / KiN

egg　ไข่　KI

electricity　ไฟฟ้า　FI-Fah

elevator　ลิฟท์　LiP

e-mail　อีเมลย์　(E-mail as in English)

embassy　สถานทูต　Sah-TooN-Toot

emergency　เหตุฉุกเฉิน　HeT-CHook-CHən

England　ประเทศอังกฤษ　P̲Bah-TeT-ahNG-GBEET

English　อังกฤษ　ahNG-GBEET

Enough!　พอ!　Po

entrance　ทางเข้า　TahNG-Kow

envelope　ซองจดหมาย　SoNG-JoT-MI

evening　ตอนเย็น　T̲oN-YeN

everything　ทุกสิ่ง　Took-SiNG

excellent ยอดเยี่ยม   YOBT-Y@@M

Excuse me. (I'm sorry.)   ขอโทษ   KO-TOT

exit   ทางออก   T@hNG-OK

expensive   แพง   P@NG

eye   ตา   T@h

eye drops   ยาหยอดตา   Y@h-YOD-T@h

F

face   ใบหน้า   BO-N@@

far   ไกล   GLO

fare   ค่าโดยสาร   K@h-DOy-S@N

fast   เร็ว   R@@u

father   พ่อ   PO

fax, fax machine   แฟกซ์, เครื่องแฟกซ์
   KB@@hNG F@K

February   เดือนกุมภาพันธ์   D@@N K@@M-P@h-P@hN

fee   ค่าธรรมเนียม   K@h-T@hM-N@@@M

few   น้อย   N@y

film (for camera)   ฟิล์ม   FOM

film (movie)   ภาพยนตร์   P@@P-P@h-YON

Fire! (emergency)   ไฟไหม้!   FO-MO

fire (heat)   ไฟ   FO

fire extinguisher เครื่องดับเพลิง
   KREUNG DAP-PLEUNG

first ที่หนึ่ง TEE-NEUNG

fish ปลา PLAH

flight เที่ยวบิน TEEO-BIN

florist คนขายดอกไม้ KON-KAI-DOK-MAI

flowers ดอกไม้ DOK-MAI

food อาหาร AH-HAN

foot เท้า TOW

fork ส้อม SOM

french fries เฟร็นช์ฟราย FREN FRAI

fresh (fruit) สด SOD

fresh (freshly cooked) สดใหม่ SOD-MAI

Friday วันศุกร์ WAN-SOOK

fried ผัด PAT

friend เพื่อน PEUAN

fruit ผลไม้ PON-LAH-MAI

funny ตลก TAH-LOK

G

gas (petrol) น้ำมันเบนซิน NAM-MAN-BEN-SIN

gas station ปั๊มน้ำมัน PAM NAM-MAN

gate ประตู PRah-Too

gift ของขวัญ KONG-KWahN

girl เด็กสาว DeK-Sow

glass (drinking) แก้ว Gaou

glasses (eye) แว่นตา WahN-Tah

gloves ถุงมือ TooNG-Mou

go (to) ไป PI

gold (color) ทองคำ TONG-KahM

golf กอล์ฟ GORP

golf course สนามกอล์ฟ Sah-NahM GOP

good ดี DEE

good-bye ลาก่อน Lah-GON

grape องุ่น ahN-GooN

grateful ภูมิใจ PooM JI

grey สีเทา SEE-Tow

green สีเขียว SEE-KEEO

grocery store ร้านขายของชำ
  BahN-KO-KONG-CHahM

guide ไกด์ GI

H

hair ผม POM

hairbrush แปรงหวีผม PRANG-WEE-POM

haircut การตัดผม GAN-TAT-POM

ham แฮม HAM

hand มือ MOU

happy ความสุข KWAM-SOOK

have (to) มี MEE

he เขา KOW

head หัว HOOah

headache ปวดหัว POOahT-HOOah

health club ชมรมสุขภาพ
CHOM-ROM SOO-Kah-PahP

heart หัวใจ HOOah-JI

heart condition โรคหัวใจ ROK HOOah-JI

heat ความร้อน KWAM-RON

hello (man speaking) สวัสดี Sah-WahD-DEE-KRahP

hello (woman speaking) สวัสดี Sah-WahD-DEE-Kah

Help! ช่วยด้วย! CHOOI-DOOI

holiday วันหยุด WahN-YooT

hospital โรงพยาบาล ROONG Pah-Yah-BahN

hotel โรงแรม ROONG-RAM

hour ชั่วโมง CHOOah-MONG

how อย่างไร Y@NG-B①

Hurry up! รีบ รีบ! B@P-B@P

husband สามี S@-M@

I

I ผม P@M (m)

I ดิฉัน D①-CH@N (f)

ice น้ำแข็ง N@M-K@NG

ice cream ไอติม ①-T①M

ill ป่วย P@①

important สำคัญ S@M-K@N

indigestion อาหารไม่ย่อย @-H@N-M①-Y@

information ข้อมูล K①-M@N

internet (same as in English) อินเตอร์เนต

interpreter ล่าม L@M

J

jacket เสื้อกันหนาว S@ah-G@N-N@

jam แยม Y@M

January เดือนมกราคม
  D@@N M@-G@-B@-K@M

jewelry เครื่องเพชรพลอย KB@NG-P@T-PL@

job งาน NY@N

juice น้ำผลไม้ NAM-PON-LAh-MI

July เดือนกรกฎาคม
DuahN Gah-Bah-Gah-Dah-KOM

June เดือนมิถุนายน DuahN MI-Too-Nah-YON

K

ketchup ซอสมะเขือเทศ SOT-MAh-Kuah-TeT

key ลูกกุญแจ LOK-GON-Ja

kiss จูบ JooP

knife มีด MeeD

know (I) รู้ Roo

L

ladies (restroom) ห้องน้ำหญิง
HONG-NAhM-YeeNG

lady ผู้หญิง Poo-YeeNG

lake ทะเลสาบ Tah-Le-SahP

language ภาษา Pah-Sa

large ใหญ่ YI

late ช้า CHAh

laundry ซักผ้า SAhK-Pah

lawyer ทนายความ Tah-NI KWAhM

left (direction) ทางซ้าย TAhNG-SI

leg ขา Kah

lemon มะนาว Mah-Now

lemonade น้ำมะนาว Nahm-Ma-Now

less น้อยกว่า Noy-GWah

letter จดหมาย Jot-Mi

lettuce ผักกาดหอม Pahk-Gaht-HOM

light ไฟ Fi

like (I) ชอบ CHOP

lips ริมฝีปาก BOM-Fee-Pahk

lipstick ลิปสติก LOP-Sah-TIK

little (amount) นิดหน่อย NiT-Noy

little (size) น้อย Noy

lobster กุ้งมังกร GOONG-Mahng-GON

long ยาว Yow

lost หาย HO

love รัก Bahk

luck โชค CHOK

luggage กระเป๋าเดินทาง GBah-Pow-DUN-Tahng

lunch อาหารกลางวัน ah-Hon-GLahng-Wahn

M

maid พนักงานทำความสะอาด
P@h-N@K-NY@N-T@hM-KW@M-S@h-@hT

mail จดหมาย J@T-M@

makeup เครื่องสำอางค์ KR@@NG S@M-@hNG

man ผู้ชาย P@@-CH@

map แผนที่ P@N-T@@

March เดือนมีนาคม D@@@hN M@-N@h-K@M

market ตลาด T@h-L@hT

match (light) ไม้ขีดไฟ M@-K@@T-F@

May เดือนพฤษภาคม
D@@@hN PR@@T-S@h-P@h-K@M

mayonnaise มายองเนส M@h-Y@NG-N@T

meal มื้ออาหาร M@@@h-H@N

meat เนื้อ N@@@h

mechanic ช่างเครื่อง CH@NG KR@@NG

meeting การประชุม G@N PR@h-CH@@M

men's (restroom) ห้องน้ำชาย
H@NG-N@hM-CH@

menu รายการอาหาร B@-G@N-@h-H@N

message ข้อความ K@B-KW@M

milk น้ำนม N@hM-N@M

mineral water   น้ำแร่   N@hM-B@

minute   นาที   N@h-T@@

Miss   นางสาว   N@hNG-S@w

mistake   ความผิดพลาด   KW@hM-P@T-PL@T

Monday   วันจันทร์   W@hN-J@hN

money   เงิน   NY@N

month   เดือน   D@w@hN

monument   อนุเสาวรีย์   @h-N@@-S@h-W@h-B@@

more   อีก   @@K

morning   ตอนเช้า   T@BN-CH@w

mosque   มัสยิด   M@hT-S@h-Y@T

mother   แม่   M@

mountain   ภูเขา   P@@-K@w

movies   ภาพยนตร์   P@P-P@h-Y@N

Mr.   นาย   N@

Mrs.   นาง   N@hNG

museum   พิพิธภัณฑ์   P@-P@T-T@h-P@hN

mushroom   เห็ด   H@T

music   ดนตรี   T@N-DB@@

mustard   มัสตาร์ด   M@hT-S@h-T@hT

N

nail clippers มีดตัดเล็บ MEET TaT LEP

name ชื่อ CHU

napkin ผ้าเช็ดปาก PA-CHET-PaK

near ใกล้ GLO

necessary จำเป็น JaM-PEN

need (to) ต้องการ TONG-GaN

never ไม่เคย MO-KUUi

news stand ที่ขายหนังสือพิมพ์
   TEE KO NaNG-SU-PIM

newspaper หนังสือพิมพ์ NaNG-SU-PIM

night คืน KUN

nightclub ไนท์คลับ NI-KLaP

no ไม่ MO

non smoking ไม่สูบบุหรี่ MO SUP Boo-REE

noon เที่ยงวัน TEEaNG-WaN

north ทิศเหนือ TIT-NUa

November เดือนพฤศจิกายน
   DUaN PROT-Sa-JEE-Ga-YON

now เดี๋ยวนี้ DEEO-NEE

number หมายเลข MO-LEK

nurse นางพยาบาล NaNG-Pa-Ya-BaN

O

occupied ไม่ว่าง   MI-WahNG

ocean มหาสมุทร   Mah-Hah-Sah-MooT

October เดือนตุลาคม   Douahn Too-Lah-KOM

office สำนักงาน   SOM-NahK NYahN

oil น้ำมัน   NahM-MahN

omelet ไข่เจียว   KI-JEEO

one-way (ticket) เที่ยวเดียว   TEEO DEEO

onion หัวหอม   Hooah HOM

online ออนไลน์   (same as in English)

open เปิด   PurT

opera อุปรากรณ์   ooP-Pah-Bah-GON

operator (phone) พนักงานโทรศัพท์
   Pah-NahK-NYahN TO-Bah-SahP

orange (color) สีส้ม   SEE-SOM

order (to) สั่ง   SahNG

original ดั้งเดิม   DahNG-Doum

owner เจ้าของ   Jow-KONG

oysters หอยนางรม   Hoy-NahNG-BOM

P

package ห่อ   HO

page หน้า N⍟

pain เจ็บ / ปวด JℰB / PₒₒₐₕT

painting ภาพเขียน P⍟P-K⍟⍟N

paper กระดาษ GBₐₕ-DₐₕT

parking lot (car) ที่จอดรด Tℰℰ-JₐₕD B⍟T

partner หุ้นส่วน H⍟⍟N-S⍟⍟ₐₕN

party งานปาร์ตี้ NYₐₕN-Pₐₕ-Tℰℰ

pass ผ่าน PₐₕN

passenger ผู้โดยสาร P⍟-D⍟ᵥ-S⍟N

passport หนังสือเดินทาง NₐₕNG-S⍟-D⍟N-TₐₕNG

pasta เส้น S⍟N

pastry ขนม Kₐₕ-N⍟M

pen ปากกา PₐₕK-Gₐₕ

pencil ดินสอ D⍟N-S⍟

pepper พริกไท PB⍟K-T⍟

perfume น้ำหอม NₐₕM-H⍟M

person คน K⍟N

pharmacist เภสัชกร P⍟-SₐₕT-CHₐₕ-G⍟N

pharmacy ร้านขายยา BₐₕN-K⍟-Yₐₕ

phone book สมุดโทรศัพท์ Sₐₕ-M⍟T T⍟-Bₐₕ-SₐₕP

photo ภาพถ่าย P⍟P-T⍟

photographer ช่างถ่ายภาพ CHⓐNG-T①-Pⓐ⃝P

pillow หมอน MⓄN

pink สีชมพู Sⓔ⃝-CHⓄM-Pⓞⓞ

plate จาน Jⓐ⃝N

plastic พลาสติก PLⓐ⃝T-Sⓐ⃝-TⓔⓔK

pocket กระเป๋าเสื้อ GRⓐ⃝-Pⓞ⃝-Sⓤ⃝ⓐ⃝

police ตำรวจ Tⓐ⃝M-Rⓞⓞⓐ⃝D

police station สถานีตำรวจ
 Sⓐ⃝-Tⓐ⃝-Nⓔⓔ Tⓐ⃝M-Rⓞⓞⓐ⃝D

pork เนื้อหมู Nⓞⓤⓐ⃝-Mⓞⓞ

porter คนขนของ KⓄN-KⓄN-KⓄNG

post office ที่ทำการไปรษณีย์
 Tⓔⓔ-Tⓐ⃝M-Gⓐ⃝N-PR①-Sⓐ⃝-Nⓔⓔ

postcard ไปรษณียบัตร PR①-Sⓐ⃝-Nⓔⓔ-Yⓐ⃝-Bⓤ⃝T

potatoes มันฝรั่ง Mⓐ⃝N-Fⓐ⃝-Rⓐ⃝NG

pregnant ตั้งครรภ์ Tⓐ⃝NG-Kⓤ⃝N

prescription ใบสั่งยา B①-Sⓐ⃝NG-Yⓐ⃝

price ราคา Rⓐ⃝-Kⓐ⃝

profit กำไร Gⓐ⃝M-B①

public telephone โทรศัพท์สาธารณะ
 T①-Rⓐ⃝-Sⓐ⃝P Sⓐ⃝-Tⓐ⃝-Rⓐ⃝-Nⓐ⃝

public toilet ห้องน้ำสาธารณะ
HONG-NahM   Sah-Tah-Rah-Nah

purple สีม่วง   SEE-Moo-ahNG

purse กระเป๋าถือ   GRah-Poo-Tou

Q

quality คุณภาพ   KooN-Nah-PaP

question คำถาม   KahM-TahM

quick เร็ว   REoo

quit (to) ลาออก / เลิก   Lah-oRK / LUK

quiet! (be) เงียบ   NGEEahP

R

radio วิทยุ   WiT-Tah-Yoo

railway station สถานีรถไฟ   Sah-Tah-NEE-RoT-FI

rain ฝน   FON

raincoat เสื้อกันฝน   Soo-ah-GahN-FON

ramp ทางลาด   TahNG-LaT

razor blades ใบมีดโกน   BI-MET-GON

ready พร้อม   PROM

receipt ใบเสร็จ   BI-SeT

recommend (I) แนะนำ   Nah-NahM

red สีแดง   SEE-DahNG

refund   เงินคืน   NYOON-KOON

reservation   การจอง   GAHN-JONG

restaurant   ร้านอาหาร   BAHN-ah-HAN

return   ไปกลับ   PI-GLAP

rice (cooked)   ข้าว   KOW

rich   รวย   BOOI

right (correct)   ถูก   TOOK

right (direction)   ขวา   KWA

road   ถนน   TAH-NON

room   ห้อง   HONG

round trip   ไปกลับ   PI GLAP

S

sad   เศร้า   SOW

safe (hotel)   ตู้เซฟ   TOO-SAF

salad   สลัด   SAH-LAHT

sale   ลดราคา   LOT-BAH-KAH

salmon   ปลาแซลมอน   PLAH-SAHL-MON

salt   เกลือ   GLOUAH

sanitary napkin   ผ้าอนามัย   PAH-ah-NAH-MI

Saturday   วันเสาร์   WAHN-SOW

scissors   กรรไกร   GAHN-GBI

sculpture (art) รูปปั้น ROOP PAN

seafood อาหารทะเล ah-HAN-TA-Le

season ฤดู ROO-DOO

seat ที่นั่ง TEE-NANG

secretary เลขานุการ Le-KA-NOO-GAhN

September เดือนกันยายน DOUAN GAN-Yah-YON

service การบริการ GAN-BO-REE-GAN

several หลาย LAI

shampoo ยาสระผม Yah-Sah-POM

sheets (bed) ผ้าปูที่นอน PA-POO-TEE-NON

shirt เสื้อเชิ้ต SUAh-SHUT

shoe shop ร้านขายรองเท้า RAhN-KAI RONG-Tow

shoes รองเท้า RONG-Tow

shopping center ห้างสรรพสินค้า
    HANG SAhP-Pah-SON-KAh

shower ฝักบัว FAhK-BOOah

shrimp กุ้ง GONG

sick ป่วย POOA

sign (display) ป้าย PAI

signature ลายเซ็นต์ LAI-SEN

single โสด SOT

sister (older / younger)   พี่สาว / น้องสาว
   PEE-SOW   /   NONG-SOW

size   ขนาด   Kah-NahT

skin   ผิวหนัง   POW-NANG

skirt   กระโปรง   GRah-PBONG

slice   เฉือน   CHOOAN

slowly   อย่างช้า   YahNG-CHah

small   เล็ก   LEK

smile (I)   ยิ้ม   YEEM

smoke (I)   บุหรี่   Boo-BEE

smoke (fire)   สูบ   SOOB

soap   สบู่   Sah-Boo

socks   ถุงเท้า   TONG-TOW

someone   คนหนึ่ง   KON-Noung NG

something   สิ่งหนึ่ง   SEENG-Noung NG

sometimes   บางครั้ง   BahNG-KRahNG

soon   เร็วเร็วนี้   BEEou BEEou NEE

sorry (excuse me)   ฉันขอโทษ   CHON KO-TOT

soup   น้ำซุป   NahM-SOOP

south   ทิศใต้   TOT-DO

souvenir   ของที่ระลึก   KONG-TEE-Bah-LOK

Spanish (language) ภาษาเสปน PAH-SAN-SAH-PEN

Spanish (person) คนเสปน KON-SAH-PEN

Spain ประเทศเสปน PRAH-TET-SAH-PEN

speed ความเร็ว KWAHM-REOU

spoon ช้อน CHON

sport กีฬา GEE-LAH

spring (season) ฤดูใบไม้ผลิ ROO-DOO-BI-MI-PLI

stamp แสตมป์ SAH-TAM

station สถานี SAH-TAN-NEE

steak เนื้อเสต็ก NOUAH SAH-TEK

Stop! หยุด! YOOT

storm พายุ PAH-YOO

straight ahead ตรงไป TRONG PI

strawberry ลูกสตรอเบอร์รี่ SAH-TAH-BUR-BEE

street ถนน TAH-NON

string เชือก CHUUAHK

subway รถไฟใต้ดิน ROT-FI-TI-DIN

sugar น้ำตาล NAHM-TAN

suit (clothes) ชุดสูท CHOOT-SOOD

suitcase กระเป๋าเดินทาง GRAH-PO-DOUN-TANG

summer ฤดูร้อน ROO-DOO-RON

sun พระอาทิตย์ / ดวงอาทิตย์
  PRah-ah-TⓘT / DooNG-ah-TⓘT

sunblock ครีมกันแดด KREEM-Gah-N-Dah-T

Sunday วันอาทิตย์ WahN-ah-TⓘT

sunglasses แว่นกันแดด WæN-Gah-N-Dah-T

supermarket ซุปเปอร์มาเก็ต SooP-Pæ-Mah-GⓔT

surprise ความประหลาดใจ KWah-M-PRah-Lah-T-Jⓘ

sweet หวาน WahN

swim (l) ว่ายน้ำ Wⓘ-Nah-M

swimming pool สระว่ายน้ำ Sah-Wⓘ-Nah-M

Synagogue สุเหร่ายิว Soo-Row-Yæ

T

table โต๊ะ <u>T</u>Ⓞ

tampon ผ้าอนามัยแบบสอด
  Pæ-ah-Nah-Mⓘ-Bâh-B-Sah-D

tasty อร่อย ah-Roy

tax ภาษี Pah-SEE

taxi รถแท็กซี่ RⓄT TâK-SEE

tea น้ำชา Nah-M-CHah

telephone โทรศัพท์ TⓄ-Rah-Sah-P

television โทรทัศน์ TⓄ-Rah-Tah-T

temperature (fever) มีไข้ MEE-KI

temperature (weather) อุณหภูมิ ooN-Hah-PooM

temple วัด Wah T

tennis เทนนิส TEN-NiT

tennis court สนามเทนนิส Sah-NaM TEN-NiT

thank you ขอบคุณ KahP KHooN

that นั่น NaN

theater (movie) โรงหนัง BONG NaNG

there ที่นั่น TEE-NaN

they พวกเขา PooK-Kow

this นี้ NEE

thread เส้นด้าย SEN-DI

throat คอหอย KO-HOY

Thursday วันพฤหัสบดี
  WaN-Pah-Boo-HaT-Sah-BO-DEE

ticket ตั๋ว Too ah

time เวลา WEB-Lah

tip (gratuity) เงินทิป NYooN TiP

tired เหนื่อย NooA

toast (bread) ขนมปังปิ้ง Kah-NOM-Pah NG-PeNG

tobacco ยาเส้น Yah-SEN

today วันนี้ WahN-NEE

toe นิ้วเท้า New-Tow

together ด้วยกัน DooA-GahN

toilet ห้องน้ำ HONG-NahM

toilet paper กระดาษชำระ GRah-DahT CHahM-Bah

tomato มะเขือเทศ Mah-Kooah-TeT

tomorrow พรุ่งนี้ PRONG-NEE

toothache ปวดฟัน PooahT-FuhN

toothbrush แปรงสีฟัน PRahNG-SEE-FuhN

toothpaste ยาสีฟัน Yah-SEE-FuhN

toothpick ไม้จิ้มฟัน MI-JOM-FuhN

tour ทัวร์ Tooah

tourist นักท่องเที่ยว NahK-TONG-TEO

towel ผ้าเช็ดตัว Pah-CHeT-Tooah

train รถไฟ BOT-FI

travel agency บริษัทท่องเที่ยว BO-BEE-SahT TONG TEO

traveler's check เช็คเดินทาง CHeK DooN-TahNG

trip เที่ยว / เดินทาง TEO / DooN-TahNG

Tuesday วันอังคาร WahN-ahNG-KahN

turkey ไก่งวง GI-NYooahNG

U

umbrella ร่ม ROM

understand (to) เข้าใจ KOW-JI

underwear กางเกงใน GANG-GĒNG NI

United Kingdom สหราชอาณาจักร
Sah-Hah-ROT-CHah-ah-Nah-Jahk

United States ประเทศสหรัฐเอมริกา
Pah-TĒT-Sah-Hah-Rah-ah-MĒ-RI-Gah

university มหาวิทยาลัย Mah-Hah-WIT-Tah-Yah-LI

up ขึ้น KON

urgent ด่วน Doo-ahN

V

vacant ว่าง WONG

vacation พักร้อน Pah-K-RON

valuable มีค่า MĒ-Kah

value ราคา Rah-Kah

vanilla วนิลา Wah-NĒ-LA

veal เนื้อลูกวัว Nou-ah-LO-K-Woo-ah

vegetables ผัก Pah-K

view ทิวทัศน์ Tew-Tah-T

vinegar น้ำส้มสายชู Nah-M-SOM-SI-CHoo

vitamins วิตะมิน WĒ-Tah-MON

W

Wait! รอ! B⊙

waiter (I need the waiter) พนักงานเสิร์ฟชาย
Pⓐh-NⓐK-NYⓐN-SⓤB CH⓪

waitress (I need the waitress) พนักงานเสิร์ฟหญิง
Pⓐh-NⓐK-NYⓐN-SⓤB YⓔNG

want (I) ต้องการ T⓪NG-GⓐN

wash (I) ล้าง LⓐNG

water น้ำ NⓐM

watermelon แตงโม TⓐNG-M⓪

we เรา B⓪w

weather อากาศ ⓐh-GⓐT

Wednesday วันพุธ WⓐN-P⓪⓪T

week อาทิตย์ / สัปดาห์ ⓐh-T⓪T / SⓐP-Dⓐh

weekend วันเสาร์อาทิตย์ WⓐN S⓪w ⓐh-T⓪T

welcome ยินดีต้อนรับ Y⓪N Dⓔ T̲⓪N-BⓐP

well done (cooked) สุกมาก S⓪⓪K MⓐK

west ทิศตะวันตก T⓪T-T̲ⓐ-WⓐN-T̲⓪K

wheelchair รถเข็น B⓪T-KⓔN

When? เมื่อไร? Mⓔⓐh-B⓪

Where? ที่ไหน? Tⓔⓔ-N⓪

Which? อันไหน? ⓐN-N⓪

white สีขาว SEE-Kow

Who? ใคร? KRI

Why? ทำไม? TahM-MI

wife ภรรยา PahN-Rah-Yah

wind ลม LOM

window หน้าต่าง Nw-TahNG

wine ไวน์ WI

winter ฤดูหนาว Roo-Too-Now

with กับ GahP

woman ผู้หญิง Poo-YENG

wonderful ดีเยี่ยม DEE-YooM

world โลก LOK

wrong ผิด PiT

XYZ

year ปี PEE

yellow สีเหลือง SEE-LooahNG

yes ใช่ CHI

yesterday เมื่อวาน Mooah-WahN

you คุณ KHooN

zipper ซิป SiP

zoo สวนสัตว์ SooahN-SahT

THANKS!

The nicest thing you can say to anyone in any language is "Thank you." Try some of these languages using the incredible EPLS Vowel Symbol System.

Spanish	French
GRah-SEE-ahS	MÊR-SEE

German	Italian
DahN-Kuh	GRahT-SEE-ê

Japanese	Chinese
DO-MO	SHEEê SHEEê

Arabic	Greek
SHoo-KRahN	êF-Hah-REE-STO

Portuguese	Hawaiian
O-BREE-Gah-DO	Mah-Hah-LO

INDEX

QUICK REFERENCE PAGE

Hello

สวัสดี

S@h-W@h-D-D@E

How are you?

สบายดีไหม?

S@h-B① D@E M②

Yes

ใช่

CH②

No

ไม่

M②

Please

ช่วย

CH⊚①

Thank you

ขอบคุณ

K@P KH⊚N

I'm sorry. / Excuse me.

ฉันขอโทษ

CH@N K⊙-T⊙T

Help!

ช่วยด้วย!

CH⊚①-D⊚①

Do you speak English?

คุณพูดภาษาอังกฤษได้ไหม?

KH⊚N P⊚ P@h-S@h

@NG-GR①T D② M②

(♂ KR@P ♀ K@h)